PENGUIN PLAYS

THE MAROWITZ HAMLET
AND
THE TRAGICAL HISTORY OF DR FAUSTUS

CHARLES MAROWITZ was born in New York City. He arrived in London in 1956 and started London's first method-school, 'The Method Workshop', in 1958. He was assistant director to Peter Brook on the Brook–Scofield *King Lear*, and co-directed the Royal Shakespeare Experimental Group in the Theatre of Cruelty Season with him. He has had numerous West End productions, the most notable among these being Joe Orton's *Loot*, Saul Bellow's *The Bellow Plays*, John Herbert's *Fortune and Men's Eyes*. In 1968 he started the Open Space Theatre, where he is now artistic director. Charles Marowitz is drama critic for the *Village Voice* and the *New York Times*.

The Marowitz Hamlet
&
The Tragical History of Dr Faustus

*

A COLLAGE VERSION OF
SHAKESPEARE'S PLAY
AND
A FREE ADAPTATION OF
MARLOWE'S PLAY

*

CHARLES MAROWITZ

PENGUIN BOOKS

Penguin Books Ltd, Harmondsworth, Middlesex, England
Penguin Books Inc., 7110 Ambassador Road, Baltimore, Maryland 21207, U.S.A.
Penguin Books Australia Ltd, Ringwood, Victoria, Australia

—

The Marowitz Hamlet first published by Allen Lane The Penguin Press 1968
Published in Penguin Plays 1970
The Tragical History of Dr Faustus first published in Penguin Plays 1969

—

The Marowitz Hamlet copyright © Charles Marowitz, 1968
The Tragical History of Dr Faustus copyright © Charles Marowitz, 1969

—

Made and printed in Great Britain by
C. Nicholls & Company Ltd
Set in Monotype Garamond

CONTENTS

The Marowitz Hamlet

*

INTRODUCTION

No work of criticism that does not take into account the fact that *Hamlet* has been around for about 400 years can begin to talk sense about what the play means to modern audiences. The critical canon is interminable, and almost every treatise on the play begins with a long- or short-winded apology for adding to a subject which, like Love or God, has, through over-elaboration, become permanently ambiguous. Being neither a scholar nor a critic, I couldn't enter into that fray even if I wanted to. In fact, writing anything at all about *Hamlet* immediately induces a sense of playing the impostor, because a director, like a playwright, is supposed to say what he means in his work and leave speculation to that peculiar breed of niggling intellectual which actually enjoys picking at the chicken-bones of art in order to re-create a semblance of the whole bird. So let me present my credentials from the outset – or rather my lack of them. I write as a director who, by dint of being one, must assemble and transmit the ideas he entertains about the material in his hands. The observations which follow are only rough indications of personal attitudes towards the play and the present reworking of it.

FIVE QUESTIONS AND A PROPOSITION

1. If one could see into Hamlet's mind, into the mind, that is, of a young man who returns home to find his father dead, his mother remarried, a ghost urging him to murder, a Court full of treachery, a State threatened by invasion, and every imaginable pressure forcing him towards an act he is temperamentally incapable of, what would one see?

2. Is it possible to express one's view of *Hamlet* without the crutch of narrative?

3. Is it not true that all of us know Hamlet, even those of us who have never read the play or seen it performed? Isn't there some smear of Hamlet somewhere in our collective unconscious which makes him familiar?

4. Can a play which is very well known be reconstructed and redistributed so as to make a new work of art? If *Hamlet* were a precious old vase which shattered into a thousand pieces, could one glue the pieces all together into a completely new shape and still retain the spirit of the original?

5. If Jan Kott is right and Shakespeare is our 'contemporary', why can't we speak to him in our own tone of voice, in our own rhythms, about our own concerns? Must we forever be *receiving* Shakespeare; why can't Shakespeare *receive us*?

I despise Hamlet.

He is a slob,

A talker, an analyser, a rationalizer.

Like the parlour liberal or the paralysed intellectual, he can describe every facet of a problem, yet never pull his finger out.

Is Hamlet a coward, as he himself suggests, or simply a *poseur*, a frustrated actor who *plays* the scholar, the courtier, and the soldier as an actor (a very bad actor) assumes a variety of different roles?

And why does he keep saying everything twice?

And how can someone talk so pretty in such a rotten country with the sort of work he's got cut out for him?

You may think he's a sensitive, well-spoken fellow, but, frankly, he gives me a pain in the ass.

The reactions which have grown up against both the Psychological and Historical schools of *Hamlet*-criticism are completely understandable. Obviously, if you reduce *Hamlet* to a behaviour-pattern, poetry becomes irrelevant, and metaphysical elements are explained away by Freudian or Jungian tenets; and the only way to understand *Hamlet* entirely in terms of the Elizabethan sensibility is to be entirely an Elizabethan. The great value of the Poel-Granville-Barker Elizabethan Revival was mainly technical. They discovered, quite rightly, that Shakespeare was being played too slow, and that by playing him faster the plays made more sense and were more exciting. This is a simplification of a movement that had much more than that to recommend it, but that seems to me its chief practical value. The view espoused by critics like C. S. Lewis, that one better understands the nature of Hamlet by receiving the Poem rather than analysing the Prince, ignores my very first point – that Hamlet, the Prince, the character *as played by the actor before members of an audience,* has been around for about 400 years. Our conception of Hamlet cannot help being eclectic. It is composed of first- and second-hand memories of actors like Booth, Irving, Forbes-Robertson Barrymore, Gielgud, Redgrave and Olivier. Every trait that any actor has ever emphasized in expressing his interpretation of the role is a hue in the multi-coloured image we have of the play. Every critical essay on the Dane has added complexion to that image. Where Lewis's argument falls down is that *Hamlet* is no longer the 'Poem'. The poem has been made flesh for us time and time again. *Hamlet* is a living amalgam of influences as dissimilar as those of the Elizabethan and the Victorian, the Freudian and the Artaudian. He is, quite literally, a mess; compounded of distortions, exaggerations, contradictions, all put through the strainer of time and delivered to a twentieth-century sensibility which is itself as complicated and contradictory as the long history the character has passed through.

This, for me, was the starting point. *Hamlet* the play, the structure that Shakespeare built and the sequence that Shakespeare assembled, had stopped *meaning*. One had almost stopped listening, in the way that one stops listening to an old and familiar tune after mechanically noting its strain and associations. But just as old tunes are continually being re-arranged in modern settings, so it is possible to reshape, rethink, restress, and redress old plays. And, of course, Shakespeare was doing this all the time. He was reworking and rehashing the commonplace narratives of his day; using Holinshed, Boccaccio, Surrey, Kyd, Marlowe and the others for his own purpose; taking plays, or parts of plays, and giving them a treatment directly comparable to that which modern arrangers apply to folk songs and standards. Of course, the reworking in Shakespeare's case produced unique and original creations; a synthesis and perfection of all the elements which had preceded him. But even perfection can pall with time, and 'classic' can become nothing more than a hands-off label that critics and scholars affix to their favourite works in order to try and preserve the pleasure they originally received from them. When that happens it is time for a 'classic' to be declassicized.

Hamlet, after all, is a very special case. It is the most often performed, the most widely read, the most thoroughly studied of Shakespeare's plays. It has – quite literally – been done to death. It has become a myth, compounded of misunderstandings, distortions, and contradictions. It is a man in black sprawled on a gravestone with a skull in his hands. It is a man looking fixedly at empty air. It is everyone who cannot make up his mind; who talks one way and behaves another. It is the wilful son of a vain mother, and the misunderstood stepson of an unsympathetic stepfather. It is the angry young man flouting conventions, and the cool hipster tuned into Zen contemplation and eschewing violence. It is the LSD tripper floating free on his 'expanded consciousness'.

It is the man caught between psychological uncertainties and moral necessities; the man who is provoked by Vietnam and paralysed by Vietnam, terrified by the Bomb and committed to the Bomb; the man weighted with the knowledge that in a corrupt world, whether one acts honourably or not at all, harm is done and corruption grows.

All of these *pertinences* are in the play, but not demonstrable because the play is imprisoned in its narrative. The play *is* the story, and to present 'the play' is to retell the story. No matter what the interpretation, it must be expressed through the narrative-line, through the progressive fiction of the play's given situations. And it is this relentless *narrativeness*, this impregnable closed circuit of story-lines, which constricts the power and suggestiveness of what the play has become. Once the narrative sequence is broken, one has direct access to the play's ambiences. One rips open the golden lid of the treasure chest to find other riches within. After a rapid inventory there is nothing to prevent one from closing the lid once more. A spliced-up *Hamlet* doesn't destroy the play forever; just as a beautiful woman who is raped isn't barred from future domestic felicity. One might argue she is never the same woman afterwards, but is that necessarily a bad thing?

For me, the crucial question about Hamlet was not: how mad or how sane, how reflective or how active? but: is it possible, today, to sit through the play as Shakespeare wrote it and still respond to its story and structure? The play has become, like a well-worn violin concerto or an opera, a test for virtuosity – either the actor's or the director's. We wait to see what Actor X will do with the big soliloquies or Director Z with the battlement scenes. If the actor is an Olivier or the director a Guthrie, we usually get our money's worth. We are given something 'different' and therefore stimulating, but are we being given the original artistic totality? Are we being

13

moved or impressed by the fable as Shakespeare wrote it?

A good director or actor can, through original interpretation, reorganize the meaning of the play so as to give it unexpected relevance. When Orson Welles gives us a fascist-dress *Julius Caesar*, he is using sixteenth-century language in order to convey a twentieth-century attitude, and the compatibility of these two seemingly disparate elements captivates us. When Peter Brook gives us a bleak, remorseless *King Lear* unfolding in a world without god or purpose, he is using a Shakespearian text to convey a contemporary state of mind in a way that reinforces both the new conception and the old work.

We all snicker at eighteenth-century 'improvements' which distorted Shakespeare's plays – even to the extent of reprieving doomed heroes and rewriting the poetry – but this was the age asking art to reflect it and baulking when it did not. As an attitude, it is quite defensible. When Brook chops out the servant scenes after Gloucester's blinding, he is doing something very similar: not crass bowdlerization but deliberate editing in order to express a personalized view of the whole. The magical property of a masterpiece is that it can be made to *mean* again even when a society no longer thinks the way its author did at the time of writing.

Directors have been finding 'new meanings' in the works of Shakespeare for centuries. No one questions any longer the director's right to reinterpret a classical work according to his own lights; to change its period, place a new emphasis on certain characters or relationships, or even, as Brecht did, rewrite plays in order to drive home one implicit idea at the expense of all others. It is this free and easy attitude to Shakespeare which has provided productions as remarkable as Guthrie's Ascot-dress *Troilus and Cressida*, Littlewood's First World War *Macbeth*, and Barton-and-Hall's amended and supplemented version of the Histories. But what has remained sacrosanct in Shakespeare is the language, the structure and the narrative. One of the questions behind the present under-taking is to discover to what extent one can juggle *those* elements and still maintain contact with what is essential in *Hamlet*.

I do not contend that all Shakespeare's plays are susceptible to the treatment which has here been given to *Hamlet*. As I say elsewhere, one of the prerequisites for Shakespearian collage is the audience's general familiarity with the play. In the case of *Hamlet* one has the added advantage of a play with a mythic base which gives an audience an even wider though less explicit frame of reference. I think the same would apply in the cases of *Macbeth*, *Othello*, and possibly *King Lear*, and be quite inapplicable to the Comedies or Histories.

For centuries, the nobility of *Hamlet* the poem has been confused with the man himself. It is possible for a man to make eloquent speeches and still be a weakling and a coward, to have intellectual perceptions and moral insights and still be made of wax. Remove the romantic aura that surrounds Hamlet, the Renaissance Prince, the man of heightened sensitivity, and look at him in cold blood and the story of the play is quite different.

Hamlet, an aristocrat-playboy who prefers amateur dramatics to ruling a kingdom, returns home after his father died under mysterious circumstances. Now that the rightful heir is back, everyone expects him to deal with a situation that cries out for remedy. Knowing he is not equal to these expectations, Hamlet desperately tries to adopt an acceptable social stance. A ghostly visitation from his dead father con-firms what he already suspected, but since it prods him into the kind of direct action he is incapable of he decides to dispute the legitimacy of the apparition. Instinctively, he feigns madness. Madness is the conventional escape route for human problems. The madman is not expected to cope, and nobody blames him. But Hamlet's rationalization is that this cunning trick will make it easier to ascertain his step-father's guilt, a contention he could never justify but which, fortunately, no one asks him to.

Incapable of real action, he sets about doing what he does best: preparing an amateur entertainment. Buoyed up by its success (the King's guilt confirmed), he encounters Claudius at prayer. Reality sobers up fantasy, and he realizes he is being given an opportunity to fulfil his father's command and still derive some honour from the deed. But he rationalizes yet another delay and, instead, decides to take on his mother, who is easier to handle. Being both a bungler and a hypocrite, he stabs the concealed Polonius, hoping he is the King but knowing full well it cannot be since he just left him at prayer. With Gertrude as a captive audience, he proceeds to work off his actor's frustrations by playing the self-righteous son admonishing the adulterous woman. Once this pose is exhausted, he gets what he really came for: the maternal bosom and a good-night kiss. Having only the corpse of Polonius as a kind of third-rate symbol for the act he should have committed, he drags it off to show the world that even if he cannot revenge the death of his father at least he can stab the vitals out of an officious old windbag hiding in ladies' closets.

Fortunately, the murder of Polonius compels him to be removed from Denmark, a decision he never disputes since he is glad of any opportunity to make tracks. He rigs the murder of two old schoolfriends not so much because they have become traitors but because, as with Polonius, the more he destroys the appendages of the King, the better he can rationalize the abrogation of the vow he made to his father.

Back in Denmark, no longer the subject of the people's expectations, a kind of ageing playboy with all his credit gone, spurned by his own countrymen, Laertes foisted in his place, Hamlet is in the last stages of disrepute. Not only will he never be Fortinbras, he will never even be Laertes. His father's command is, by this time, a longstanding broken vow. His emnity towards the King has dwindled into pique. No one, least of all Hamlet, takes it very seriously. The spectacle of Laertes' impassioned grief at Ophelia's funeral forcibly reminds Hamlet of the man he could have been. He quickly simulates a passion to show the world there is still some fight in the old war-horse, but everyone recognizes this as just another histrionic display. Gertrude, no longer the subject of a moral quarrel but simply the 'mum' of old, soothes her distracted baby.

The promise of a duel with Laertes before the Court and in the presence of the King is Hamlet's pathetic comeback chance. Here, at least, he will be able to show his mettle: to suggest that *had he wanted to wreak a terrible revenge* nothing could have stopped him. The duel, like the play scene, is a staged event, and so, naturally, he warms to it. To the end of his days, he will drone on to Horatio about 'He that hath kill'd my King and whor'd my mother'. In fact, had Hamlet lived to a ripe old age he would have become as tedious as old Yorick must have been, describing the feats he *might have* performed; aggrandizing the misadventure of Polonius's death; his sly handling of Rosencrantz and Guildenstern, etc.: a pathetic old bore given to spiritualism and nostalgia for the 'good old days' before the reign of Fortinbras.

In the duel scene, though he suspects foul play, he takes no precautions. He is almost like a man too weak for suicide hoping some accident will dispatch him. Told he has been poisoned and has only minutes to live, he flares out all over the place, finally killing the King, but in such a mindless state of panic that the act is devoid of any honour or dignity. Horatio, the 'good friend' who can be relied on not to reveal embarrassing truths, be they halitosis, body odour, or moral cowardice, lets the dying Prince play out his final role:

Death of a Hero. Desperately trying to contain a snigger, he hears Fortinbras order a soldier's funeral for this effete, aesthetic, intellectual non-starter. As for Hamlet, in his last words the two main themes of his life combine: (1) his egoism requests that Horatio go about putting out a good review of his deplorable performance; and (2) he acknowledges his total inadequacy for ever having been ruler of the kingdom and says, virtually, thank God a real man is on the way; this rotten old country needs a leader and I always knew it wasn't me – even though I couldn't say so. The rest is silence, just as the former had been cowardice, fantasy and empty bombast.

WORDS AND ACTIONS

Hamlet, like many contemporary intellectuals, equates the taking of a position with the performance of an action. He is like those zealous paraplegics who fume about Vietnam or the military takeover in Greece or the race crisis in America, and believe that the intensity of their convictions in some way affects the issue; that by trumpeting their moral righteousness to the world they are actively remedying a situation. Compare such people with the less demonstrative activists who infiltrate southern ghettos and get their heads bashed in, or risk their civilian lives supplying plasma and medicine to the wounded of Vietnam or organize Latin American conspiracies under the constant threat of imprisonment, and the pseudo-adventurousness of the 'intellectual position' is woefully revealed.

Like these armchair-commandos, Hamlet brilliantly defines his private and public dilemma; what has happened; what it portends; what must be done about it. The paralysis which ensues is delightful because it enables him to indulge both his fantasy and his masochism. That is, he glories in having an important job to do and lashes himself for not being up to it. He feeds on the violence seething in his mind and asks for nothing more than its delicious implications. It is very much like the situation of a man who derives more satisfaction from masturbation and erotic imagery than intercourse with a real woman. After a time, no actual contact can compare with the delights of his own fancy. For Hamlet, the prospect of killing Claudius is too titillating to be obliterated by the physical act of murder, and he postpones that act the way the fornicator draws out the actions leading to orgasm, believing the longer the postponement the greater the ultimate satisfaction. Hamlet's murder of Claudius in the last scene is, compared to the speculations of 'Now he is praying And now I'll do it' and the joyful discoveries after the Play scene, utterly perfunctory. It is a delay which is not only dishonourable but also perverse. In fact, it is the perversity that makes it so dishonourable.

FORTINBRAS AND HAMLET: JEKYLL AND HYDE

Fortinbras is Hamlet; Hamlet is Fortinbras: in everything, that is, but leadership, resolution and action. When Hamlet refers to a 'delicate and tender Prince whose spirit is with divine ambition puff'd', he could use no better words to describe himself. (It is curious that Hamlet and Fortinbras never perform on the stage together. Only when Fortinbras exits does Hamlet appear, and it is only after Hamlet is dead that Fortinbras arrives. The Jekyll-Hyde parallel is fanciful rather than provable, but it reinforces the theory that Fortinbras is a kind of wish-fulfilment conjured up by Hamlet; a marvellously wrought figment who soldiers where Hamlet shirks and who reigns after Hamlet disappears.)

Hamlet needs Fortinbras: that is, a somewhat-unreal and

abstract figure to emulate and admire, because if he were to choose his models closer to home he would have to fasten on to Laertes, and that would be too humiliating. It is all right to make a hero of an unfamiliar stranger, but if you acknowledge the same virtues in one of your own generation you automatically disparage yourself. Laertes whores honestly, feels passionately, fights impulsively and speaks directly. He has all the makings of kingship. Hamlet toys with women's affections, whores furtively, prefers internal struggles to open combats, would rather rationalize than actualize his passions, and is continually in doubt as to how much he honestly feels and how much he is dramatizing. A man of straw prefers imaginary heroes to superior versions of himself.

There is very little evidence to suggest that Fortinbras is the great man Hamlet makes him out to be. Fortinbras does not act boldly against the State of Denmark as his father did. He merely 'pesters' Claudius with 'messages importing the surrender of those lands lost by his father'. When he actually arrives on the soil of Denmark, he is courteous and unbelligerent. He 'craves the conveyance of a promis'd march over his kingdom'. That is, he requests permission to move on to Poland – not for any significant battle, but to appropriate a little patch of ground 'that hath in it no profit but the name'. A small-scale colonial adventure to gain a tiny sphere of influence, and it is this act which Hamlet so aggrandizes in his next soliloquy, where he proclaims the dubious dictum: 'Rightly to be great Is not to stir without great argument But greatly to find quarrel in a straw When honour's at the stake' – a justification all imperialist powers have used in appropriating territory that doesn't belong to them. But it is not the act that impresses Hamlet – he has neither the interest nor the political awareness to understand it (a lowly captain clues him up with all the details); it is the gesture that impresses him – a readiness to play the hero; make the grandstand play; act with conviction – no matter how wrong-headed it may be (the same sort of reasoning that decides Hector and his cohorts on the Trojan War). Hamlet is more susceptible to the stance and the show than he is to the personality and the true intentions. He sees a splendidly bedecked soldier cross the stage at the head of a large army. There is pomp, power, and all its glittering trappings. Here is a subject rife for identification.

The attempt to justify this watery Wittenberg intellectual as a 'real soldier' stems from the confusions of the last scene. Horatio hits the right note when he uses feminine imagery in his eulogy to Hamlet: 'Good night sweet Prince, and flights of Angels sing thee to thy rest.' Flights of angels are really more appropriate than 'four captains' and a military funeral. It is Fortinbras, the soldier nonpareil, who trots out all the misleading military imagery; who calls for 'the soldiers' music and the rites of war'. He has just conquered in Poland; he is thick with combat; he has buried many of his own men in plundering a foreign country. A volley blast heralds his arrival at Elsinore. Not knowing the weakling the Prince of Denmark was, but seeing him in the midst of carnage, he assumes, quite wrongly, that Hamlet – like himself – was ever the man of action. Had he been around for the previous four acts, he would more likely command a patch be rooted out beside the dead Ophelia; that would really be a fitter resting-place for the milk-water prince. But Fortinbras measures everyone by his own yardstick, and the dead Hamlet benefits from the miscalculation. It is just the sort of mistake a fatuous soldier, awed by royalty, would make. The cruellest sentiment in Fortinbras's last speech is 'For he was likely, had he been put on, to have prov'd most royally'. How was Fortinbras to know that in fact he *was* 'put on' from his first encounter with the Ghost to the duel with Laertes and, in fact, prov'd most un-royally?

OPHELIA = LOLITA

I cannot think of Ophelia except erotically. Despite her primness at Court, her guarded attitude to the Prince, her upright and officious father (what kind of mother did she have, I wonder?), there is still something palpably voluptuous about her. The very first time we see her, Laertes (himself so great a rake that his father must put watches on him when he travels abroad) is urging her not to open her 'chaste treasures' to Hamlet's 'unmaster'd importunity'; an exhortation which smacks of closing stable doors after the horse has fled. Ophelia, a hipster beneath her courtly silks and laces, quite rightly shrugs off moralistic advice from a libertine whose 'primrose path' is vividly imagined by Polonius (Act II, Scene 1) leading to 'such a house of sale, *Videlicet,* a brothel or so forth'. Laertes, a well-connected youth at Court – and therefore at leisure – has done his share of whoring, and his sister, confined to filial duties, has got all the backwash. More than likely her appetites have been whetted: this ostensibly prim daughter of a leading Court councillor, continually urged to chastity, in a society brimming over with promiscuity; a world teeming with forbidden delights. Her situation is made even more delicate because the heir-apparent has taken a fancy to her, and Father is in the government. Personal inclinations are at odds with political decorum in a State already made tense by a King's sudden death and the speedy and incestuous marriage of Queen to King's brother. No sooner has Laertes told Ophelia to keep a watch on herself than her father picks up the same strain, and there is no mistaking Polonius's fear:

> Do not believe his vows, for they are brokers,
> Not of that dye which their investments show,
> But mere implorators of unholy suits,
> Breathing like sanctified and pious bawds,
> The better to beguile.

Polonius recognizes Hamlet's motives; so does Laertes, and it would be too great an insult to her female intuition to suggest Ophelia does not. Another proof that Hamlet's intentions are strictly dishonourable is that hideous love-poem that Polonius has probably browbeaten out of Ophelia, although he claims it was given him out of obedience. (Significantly, he claims it twice in quick succession.)

> To the Celestial, and my Soul's idol, the most
> beautiful Ophelia.
> Doubt thou, the Stars are fire,
> Doubt that the Sun doth move,
> Doubt Truth to be a liar,
> But never doubt, I love.

O dear Ophelia, I am ill at these numbers: I have not Art to reckon my groans; but that I love thee best, O most Best, believe it. Adieu.

Thine evermore, most dear Lady, whilst this machine is to him,
> Hamlet.

It is precisely the sort of poem a man without real passion manufactures in order to make a woman more sexually accessible. And is there anything more uncharacteristic of Hamlet than those stilted emotionless phrases?

Ophelia has certainly yielded to Hamlet before the play has begun. That is why, when she discovers her chances of marrying into royalty destroyed by Hamlet's unexpected aberrations, she feels 'of ladies most deject and wretched', having suck'd (among other things) 'the honey of his music vows'. Immediately before this speech Hamlet, raging with that feigned madness so temperamentally comfortable to psychotics that it has quite rightly created suspicions about his true sanity, has flung Ophelia's loose moral behaviour back in her face. When Hamlet cries 'Get thee to a nunnery' (i.e. whorehouse), his distaste is twofold: that he could sink to the same kind of lechery with Ophelia as his mother has committed with his stepfather, and that Ophelia should be as accessible to him as Gertrude was to Claudius. It is the classic repulsion of the lover who despises his sexual object because he discovers she is just as readily enjoyed by others. In this scene, Ophelia is the substitute for Gertrude. One scene later he will be using Ophelia as a ploy in order to taunt his mother. The sexual repugnance – essentially hypocritical but no less strong for being so – is perfectly consistent from the nunnery scene to the closet scene. Hamlet humiliates Ophelia, wanting to wound Gertrude; both being guilty (in his mind) of the same sin. In the play scene, he toys with Ophelia in order to disconcert his mother, and in the closet scene, after the emotional liberation of the play scene, he aims his hostility directly at its true object. From then on, Ophelia, her usefulness ended, no longer figures in his life. Just before she dies (her repressions having already exploded into insanity) she acknowledges her promiscuity in the bawdy songs she may now sing quite openly. She is freed of the social inhibitions enforced by father, brother, and position at the Court. Madness is her escape hatch. Quite likely, Hamlet did 'promise her to wed' before 'tumbling' her, but certainly it would never have come to pass had she 'come to his bed' or not.

None of these observations is contradicted by Hamlet's passionate outburst at Ophelia's grave. Being a psychotic, he finds it easy to convert what was once a flighty deception into a passionately held belief. He 'lov'd Ophelia', he bleats to the world; 'forty thousand brothers Could not with all their quantity of love Make up my sum.' But essentially, the scene is a kind of irrational contest with Laertes: another son of a murdered father; another contender for the crown, and in almost every respect, a stronger contender than Hamlet. When Laertes' father is killed, Laertes moves swiftly to revenge. Returned to Denmark and sensing the teeming corruption of the state, he has already organized resistance and a properly incensed mob are demanding: 'Laertes shall be King.' In every comparable situation (and many of them are identical), Laertes does what Hamlet ought to. At Ophelia's funeral, Laertes quite naturally professes love for his dead sister. Hamlet, who cannot abide any passion which is stronger than his own theatricality, construes this as a challenge, and Laertes, the honestly mourning brother, is transformed into a rival, and – irony of ironies – a rival for one that Hamlet himself never loved. The gist of his hysterics at the grave is not really about Ophelia, but about his capacity to outdo Laertes in lamentation. Laertes' feelings are simple and direct:

> Lay her i' the earth,
> And from her fair and unpolluted flesh
> May violets spring.

Hamlet's, rhetorical and false:

> Be buried quick with her, and so will I:
> And if thou prate of mountains, let them throw
> Millions of acres on us; till our ground
> Singeing his pate against the burning zone
> Make Ossa like a wart. Nay, and thou'lt mouth,
> I'll rant as well as thou.

Returned from England, memories of the English tragedians fresh in his mind, the Lord Hamlet, a blustering phony to the end.

To say that Ophelia is like Lolita is at once a distortion and an extension of certain truths about the character as Shakespeare depicts her. To see her as a Court dolly, a sexual convenience passed methodically from one peer to the other and even turning up in Claudius's bed, is, of course, untrue in terms of Shakespeare's text, but a conceivable fantasy in the mind of a man who, obsessed with images of lechery and incest, is prone to more hallucinations than Shakespeare himself might have imagined.

THE GHOST

The endless problem of the Ghost is how to make awesome something modern audiences do not take seriously. The answer, traditionally, is to try to frighten with eerie sounds, disembodied voices, and spooky lighting; devices which cheapen and reduce the significance of the Ghost.

Hamlet's father, despite all the 'ghostly' terms invoked ('apparition', 'illusion', 'goblin damn'd', etc.), is real to Hamlet, and was real to Shakespeare and credible to an Elizabethan audience. What is frightening about a ghost is not its unearthliness, but its earthliness: its semblance of reality divorced from existence.

For a man locked in a fantasy, real and unreal are meaningless terms. Everything that enters his perceptions is real *for him*. In the collage, the dead King is mixed with the living King and then again with the Player-King; the dead father with the stepfather; the faithless mother with the seeming-faithless mistress; the past with the present; the actual with the illusory. Such a mixture poses certain questions about the characters of the Kings, the live one and the dead one, which are never adequately dealt with in the play.

King Hamlet. This rasping, vengeful old codger who ruled a kingdom already rotten – for the corruption at Court certainly existed before Claudius ever came to the throne; this vindictive old shade demanding retribution from beyond the grave – not to test Hamlet's mettle, but because his son is the only means by which he can exact vengeance. He needs a living tool to do his work in the living world, and his son is the obvious choice. But what kind of king was he? Ruler of a war-torn state; advancer of toads like Polonius; husband to a vain, fickle creature like Gertrude; father of a wishy-washy son who, if he'd had either the gumption or the guile, could have been ruler after his father. How did Claudius manage – so conveniently – to pop in 'between th' election and [Hamlet's] hopes'? (One thinks of Trotsky neglecting to return to Moscow after Lenin's death while Stalin 'popp'd in between th' election' and *his* hopes.) Everything we discern about the dead king and the kingdom he bequeathed throws doubt upon his character. Horatio tells us 'this side of our known world esteem'd him valiant,' but that is a military attribute, and it is the Norwegian wars Horatio is referring to. As for his moral virtues, apart from his own biased comparison with Claudius, 'a wretch whose gifts were poor To those of mine', we have only the word of his bleating son, and we know from his behaviour with Ophelia and Gertrude how changeable *his* nature is. In fact, Hamlet is a poor judge of most people in the play – not because he is thick, but because, being the most subjective character in world drama, he lacks the objectivity to see people clearly. He honestly believes Laertes to be 'a very noble youth' and amiably disposed towards him despite the fact that he killed his father and sent his sister to distraction. Because he thinks Polonius a fool, Polonius *is* a fool when both are together, but when conducting his affairs of state or conversing with his children, there is nothing of the 'foolish prating knave' about him. Hamlet decries the moral side of Claudius's character, but from all we see Claudius is an efficient monarch and a tactful politician. The crowning irony in Hamlet's bungling misadventures is that, when he finally does dispatch the King, he leaves the country in a worse state than it ever was under Claudius: in the hands of a foreign conqueror whose father was thrashed by Hamlet's father and who has coveted the land ever since. Hamlet hands Fortinbras Denmark on a platter. The patch of ground that he went off to conquer in Poland may have had no profit in it 'but the name', but on the way back he gains an entire kingdom without so much as firing a shot. The 'damndest defeat' in the play is not Claudius's murder of the King, but the loss of an entire country due to the cantankerous neurosis of one man who wasn't up to his job.

HAMLET AS BUFFO

Rosencrantz and Guildenstern! Was ever a vaudeville team better named? And was the spirit of vaudeville ever better expressed than in exchanges like:

HAMLET:

Good lads; how do ye both?

ROSENCRANTZ:

As the indifferent children of the earth.

GUILDENSTERN:

Happy, in that we are not over-happy:

On Fortune's cap, we are not the very button.

HAMLET:

Nor the soles of her shoe?

ROSENCRANTZ:

Neither, my Lord.

HAMLET:

Then you live about her waist, or in the middle of her favours?

GUILDENSTERN:

Faith, her privates, we.

HAMLET:

In the secret parts of Fortune? Oh, most true; she is a strumpet.

The comedy in Hamlet is imbued with music-hall. The gravediggers are almost too blatantly straight-man and comic, and Osric, a satirical extravagance put in at the last moment to lighten the heavy weather of the play's finale. Even Hamlet, in his more manic moments, sinks to punnery and burlesque. In the collage, the comedy has been both concentrated and exaggerated. The two faces of Polonius have been incorporated literally. The same actor, cutting between two distinct characterizations, plays both Polonius and a character called Clown which is made up from the gravediggers' quips and cribs from other characters' speeches.

The image of the recorders is basic to Hamlet's relationship with Rosencrantz and Guildenstern, and I have tried to externalize it by showing Hamlet playing and being played upon. A jumping-rope links Rosencrantz and Guildenstern, the Bobsy Twins of Shakespearian tragedy. They are as inseparable as the front and back ends of a vaudeville horse. Hamlet manipulates the rope (or rides the horse) both to amuse himself and to indulge his cruelty. When he is with Rosencrantz and Guildenstern we catch glimpses of the prankster of Wittenberg: the instigator of university rags and the buoyant undergraduate. When he turns against them, we see the adult meting out the only revenge he successfully dispatches – although even in disposing of Rosencrantz and Guildenstern he relies on forgeries and intermediaries rather than direct personal action. Significantly, he allows them no 'shriving time' – precisely the sin he condemns in Claudius's murder of his father.

OPEN LETTER TO HORATIO

Dear Horatio,

I know the world esteems you a 'good friend', but in my opinion you are a rotter. A good friend doesn't let *his* good friend continually delude himself. A good friend says: you've got everything on your side, and if you kill the King and wrest control everyone will support you, but if you continue to indulge in amateur theatricals and walk around with your head up your arse you will lose what small dignity you still possess.

You are the most obnoxious Yes-man in the Shakespearian canon. I suspect that, at base, you are a career-opportunist. If your loquacious aristocratic schoolmate ever gains control in Denmark, your future is assured. (No doubt you have your eye on the Ministry of Education.) It isn't until the last moments that you realize you have been backing the wrong horse, and I wonder to what extent your passionate moans for the dying prince are a grandstand play for the new king. I loathe your muttering obsequiousness, your 'Aye, my lord' and 'No, my lord' and 'Is't possible, my lord?'

It is no wonder Hamlet thinks so highly of you. You possess the very same fault that cripples him: the inability to permit conviction to give birth to action. You lack the moral gumption that makes a man forsake fruitless intellectual roundabouting for the sharp, straight path of direct action. To say that your 'blood and judgement are so well com-mingled, That they are not a pipe for Fortune's finger, To sound what stop she please' is only another way of saying there is no impulse so naturally overwhelming that you would not be able to rationalize its reversal or abandonment. Not being 'Passion's slave' is one thing, but being so devoid of passion that every rapier thrust is converted to a pin-prick is just elaborate hypocrisy. It is a fancy way of saying the mind is so much the master of the heart that nothing can be truly felt that is not fully understood, and since honour is more a matter of the heart than the mind, this is just an excuse for evasion and cowardice.

The Lord Hamlet loves you for those very qualities which prove his undoing. Like you, he is one that suffers all yet suffers nothing – since sufferance that doesn't lead to remedy is suffering nothing. Like you, he takes Fortune's buffets and rewards with equal thanks. Fortune has deprived him of a kingdom; he makes no move to recover it. Fortune has besmirched the memory of his father; and amidst much breastbeating and verbosity he accepts the new dispensation. Fortune sends him to England; he goes. Fortune wafts him back; he returns. Fortune has him killed in a duel; and he *defies augury* by walking straight into the trap.

If the old adage is true and one can read people by knowing their friends, then you are an accurate gauge of Hamlet's inadequacies. I have excised you from my *Hamlet* since you simply hang around like an insufferable feed, wasting pedantry on soldiers who couldn't give a damn, and making false bravura gestures like drinking from a poisoned goblet that's already been emptied. I have, however, endowed Fortinbras with a great dollop of the Horatio you should have been in a short conversation-piece after the trial scene. I hope you will not take this too personally; but the fact is that until further notice your services will no longer be required.

HAMLET AS MYTH

The core of *Hamlet* is not to be found in the *Historia Danica* or the *Histoires Tragiques* of François de Belleforest or Kyd's *Spanish Tragedy*, but in myths so embedded in human consciousness that no one can trace them to any one source. It is because *Hamlet* is essentially *mythic* that one can weave endless variations on its theme. Shakespeare's play is itself a variation of one or several of those legends that swirl around in every country's sub-culture. I tried to remember when I first became conscious of *Hamlet*. I suppose it was at school, but I can distinctly remember *knowing Hamlet* long before it was ever trotted out as a required text; knowing it not with total knowledge of each strand in its story but in a kind of grey intuitive way; knowing its aura and its ambience rather than itself.

Professor Elphin Jones has worked out a fascinating mythic background to the play, based on the notion of the challenger-

and-the-champion: a prehistoric concept which tallies with much of its story. Loosely paraphrased this is his theory:

The origins of human society are based on the tensions between the dominant male (the bull, the stallion) and the challenging younger males. At an early stage of development, human beings did not realize that the male was involved in procreation. It appeared to them that women alone were responsible for the continuation of the species. Since women were dominant in magic (i.e. effective control of the environment), lasting power could rest only with them. They tamed the young of animals which were killed for food, and probably originated herding. The magical spirit of growth, of birth and death, was incarnate in woman. She was the fount of power, the totem of rule, the 'sacred queen'. Consequently, the young males built up, via jostling and other feats of skill, a challenge with which to win the female. Each year they fought for her favours, and the winner became her 'sacred king'. His conquest represented the strength of the tribe. At the end of the year he was sacrificed, although he might live if he defeated his challengers.

The Hamlet story, Jones believes, may be an attempt to change from a concept of kingship by marriage to the 'sacred queen' to a concept of kingship by inheritance from father to son. Viewed from this standpoint, Hamlet is refusing to accept the usurper-king, although king by marriage and putting himself forward as challenger. But by the time the Hamlet story was going through its Shakespearian permutation, the crime of incest was recognized by the community, and if Hamlet successfully challenges the usurper, he has to marry his mother to be true 'sacred king'. The overtones of the Oedipus conflict which actors and directors have 'read into' *Hamlet* is an instinctive grasping of the older myth clinging to the later one. The ambivalence in the Hamlet–Gertrude relationship exists in Shakespeare's play. It is not a 'psychological imposition'. Shakespeare, in his inspired and eclectic way, was using different strands of the same story, unavoidably mixing mythic sub-texts by 'bringing up to date' older material. Perhaps it is this mixing-up of irreconcilable myths that produced in Hamlet that 'emotion' which, according to T. S. Eliot, is 'inexpressible because it is in excess of the facts as they appear'. 'Hamlet', says Eliot, 'is up against the difficulty that his disgust is occasioned by his mother, but that his mother is not an adequate equivalent for it; his disgust envelops and exceeds her. It is thus a feeling which he cannot understand; he cannot objectify it, and it therefore remains to poison life and obstruct action. None of the possible actions can satisfy it; and nothing Shakespeare can do with the plot can express Hamlet for him. . . .' But if the *inexpressible* is the dilemma that the challenger cannot oust the usurper without committing incest through marriage with the 'sacred queen' then that is a crisis which truly cannot be objectified as it was as indiscernible to Shakespeare as it was to Hamlet.

Hamlet, in ritualistic terms, has to find a new ground for challenge, and a new myth on which to base his kingship. The new ground for challenge is retribution, justice for the murdered king, punishment for his murderers. The new basis for kingship must be the son's inheritance of the father's crown lost through treachery. This, of course, poses another problem for Hamlet and one which makes Hamlet's mythic dilemma even more 'inexpressible', for if the present King has triumphed through treachery the Queen is implicated and, if retribution follows, is sure to be discredited.

The old-king-new-king-champion-challenger tension in Hamlet may represent, in mythic terms, an attempt to change the tribe's method of creating a new king. The original Hamlet story may well have been based on a myth which either records an attempt to change the rules of kingship, or represents a myth put out as propaganda designed to create respectable reasons for a change in precedent which had already taken place. By the time the story got down to Shakespeare it was just an anecdote, on a par with fairy-tales or ancient parables. Shakespeare, in his reworking of the story, builds in a new set of tensions, conflicts derived from his own time and (probably) his own life. But the older tensions, the ones ingrained in the myths on which the stories are based, remain to haunt the sub-text and perhaps produce the 'intractable material' so many critics complain of.

The answer is not to apply unlimited scholarship to track down the sources of the play wherever in history or prehistory they may be hiding, but to accept that an old story is rooted in mysteries that never really disappear and which have to be re-jigged in order to translate effectively into the present. A cut-up version of *Hamlet*, one may contend, has nothing to do with the play Shakespeare wrote, even if it does utilize his words and many of his ideas. But one can just as readily ask to what extent Shakespeare can be counted the author of a play which is compounded of ancient group-myths and cultural *bubumeinshes* as well as being obviously culled from two or three verifiable, non-Shakespearian sources. I do not say this to belittle Shakespeare's achievement, but surely the gradations are endless. If a story is root-material plus reworking plus an author's viewpoint, then a play is all that plus directorial interpretation and the further transmutations of audience make-up, time of presentation, etc. There is a great deal in *Hamlet* which Shakespeare cannot be held accountable for but which nevertheless exists and must be dealt with in retelling the tale. When a play gets 'handed down' from generation to generation over a period of 400 years, it ends up with a great number of fingerprints on it. Smudge is part of art.

SOMEWHERE IN ELSINORE

It is a very limited view of reality which contends that a play must take place in a concrete setting; almost like saying that life 'takes place' in one's home, whereas we know that *where* we are is always a secondary consideration to who we think we are and what we happen to be feeling. We may start a job-interview in a plush, West End office but in a moment's time we are operating from some inner, indeterminate point deep in our own being which may be as threadbare as a derelict shack in a shanty town. And summoned to a hospital waiting-room to be given news of life or death, we are equally in a torture-chamber, a blind-alley, and a bottomless pit. Similarly, in *Hamlet*, the King and Queen may well be in the Court of Denmark but their son is located in an elaborate private maze threaded with doubts and resentments. Although Hamlet begins the closet scene in his mother's bedchamber, once he is immersed in painful comparisons between the dead King and his stepfather he is in some less distinguishable place, poised between the present and the past; and when the Ghost arrives on the scene, he is transferred to yet another plane, perhaps damp with cold and smelling of battlements.

Yes, you may say, but these are different states of mind that occur in every scene and change in almost every speech. Surely it is for the actor to convey all that through his art, and it is idiotic to suggest there be as many locales as there are inner shifts of character. Although that is true, the fact remains that tangible settings perpetuate physical locales when the scene has shifted to other, more significant planes. And when, for instance, the dramatic reality of a scene suggests barrenness and desolation, the sight of settings and furniture cannot be blotted out of a spectator's mind as easily as it can from the character's.

Is it not possible to use the theatre to reflect states of mind more accurately – not simply by removing settings but by implementing the space-of-the-stage so that its visual elements convey psychic moods, not only 'period' environment and physical locations? If a room could disappear on the stage at the very moment that it fades out of a character's awareness, an audience would be given a precise, dramatic indication of an internal state. If a house could reflect the transformations that a character experiences in that house, something of the permutations of our inner selves would be shown on the stage.

When we use expressions such as 'the ground opened up beneath me', 'walking on air', 'lost in the clouds', 'flipped his lid', 'knocked for a loop', 'went off his head', we are instinctively employing poetic language to convey real but indefinable inner states. It is these states the theatre must learn to convey visually.

This delineation of interior reality is second nature to the *nouveau roman* and is happening everywhere in films. In *The Red Desert*, for instance, Antonioni uses colour for its emotive rather than realistic effect. In Truffaut and Resnais, subliminal flashes are continually used to illustrate inner thoughts and provide sub-textual counterpoints to the main action. In certain Happenings in New York and Paris, members of an audience wander through environments that literally transform before their eyes. In the best of these 'events', the effect is of *being part of* the permutations happening around one. In the theatre, it would be like having a new vantage point on an emotional change, an internal rather than a topographical view of what is happening inside a character. Obviously, in a realistic play, this could be both chichi and irrelevant, but as the theatre is hightailing it away from realism, it must inevitably learn this other, newly evolving language.

I loathe theatre scenery because it is like a phonograph-record caught in a groove; it repeats itself endlessly while the play progresses. No scenery I have ever seen can keep up with the progress of a play like *Hamlet* because it really takes place in the actor's and spectator's shifting consciousness. That is the best place to stage any play. It doesn't rule out the set-designer, it simply directs him away from predetermined choices and into an area he knows very little about; an area where colour, texture, object, and shape dramatize interior rather than exterior reality; where simultaneity of visual effects produce chords as sonorous and as exciting as those in modern music.

TIPS FOR SET-DESIGNERS RE THE COLLAGE

Hamlet takes place *in* Hamlet. We see sights because they are reflected through Hamlet's sensibility. Elsinore is a figment of Hamlet's imagination; so are Gertrude, Claudius, and the Ghost. So is poetry; so is comedy; so is pleasure and pain. Hamlet's cerebrum is our cyclorama, his forehead, our proscenium arch. The recesses of Hamlet's mind are our flies. An 'interior' is not simply the 'inside of a room', but the inner perspective of the people who inhabit that room. A colour is an emotional hue. An object is as large or small, as real or fantastical, as a character's perception dictates. Ignore all textual stage-directions. Have a long drink with the actors playing the main roles. Urge them to discuss their characters; to exaggerate; to use personal imagery; to be far-fetched. Base all your choices on their instincts.

HAMLET AND DISCONTINUITY

Since films and novels use it all the time, we should be accustomed to discontinuity, but the theatre, so long in the marble clutches of Aristotle, finds it impossible to function except chronologically. Sometimes, of course, it resorts to flash-backs or flash-forwards, but these have become adjuncts to the unities, not alternatives.

The most persuasive argument against the formalism of beginning-middle-and-end is that it is not truthful. Our lives simply do not unfold like that. Their rhythms are erratic; their points of focus, varied and unpredictable; their time-structure, if not actually broken, psychologically disjointed and confused. In a time of fission, we cannot accept art that is homogeneous; not if we expect art truthfully to reflect our lives.

Life today (I am not philosophizing, merely trying to illustrate) is very much like the front page of a daily news-paper. The eye jumps from one story to another, from one geographical location to another, from one mood to another: a fire in Hoboken, an election in Paris, a coronation in Sweden, a rape in London, comedy, passion, trivia – all flooding one's consciousness almost simultaneously. The writer, however, and the actor after him with centuries of tradition behind him, moves solidly from point A to point B to point C. His characters are *established*, his relationships *develop*, his plot thickens, and his conflicts resolve. In short, he plods on in his Aristotelian way, perpetuating the stock jargon of drama and the arbitrary time-system of the con-ventional theatre.

The fundamental problem of theatrical discontinuity is communication. If you decide to tell a story about a man throwing over his wife and marrying his daughter, and decide to convey this through random and arbitrary flashes from that man's life, it is quite possible no one will understand your story. You have removed the narrative frame of reference, prevented an audience from meeting your characters and watching them develop through actions. There is no reason why they should understand sporadic flashes out of a story to which they come as strangers and of which they see nothing but disconnected bits.

And yet, disconnected bits are all we know of most peoples'
story, with the possible exception of our own. We piece
together information, hunches, guesses, lies and hearsay
about everyone we know. Our much-touted 'understanding'
of people is simply this eclectic, incomplete, second-hand
hodge-podge of poorly filtered data. In life, narrative is the
accumulation of discontinuous events spread over a long
period of time, eventually assembled into a story. Dramatic
art has, for centuries, been doing the same thing, except that
in wedging its material into a pre-existing form (Aristotelian
play-structure) it has unavoidably falsified its findings. You
cannot demonstrate a circle if all you have at your disposal
are square blocks. You *can* construct an octagonal shape and
say, well a circle is something like that, only try to imagine
all those straight edges rounded off. That is the dilemma of
the theatre today: trying with simple and inappropriate
forms to convey the elaborate content of our lives. When the
content refuses to be restricted within those forms and bursts
them apart (as in Happenings, for instance) the pundits cry:
whatever it is, it's not theatre. Of course it's not. Theatre, as
we all know, is something we can assemble within our square
blocks. Whatever is difficult to assemble may be 'experimental' or 'avant-garde', but anything that absolutely resists
assembly simply isn't theatre.

Shakespeare's *Hamlet* is a play intended for square blocks.
I am not disparaging it. It has been a very good play, and has
operated successfully within those blocks and, no doubt,
will do so again. But because it has been around so long and is
so well known, it is well suited for breaking out of those
blocks. I said before that disconnected bits are all we know of
most people's stories except our own. I should add that we
know the stories of those people whose bits have been
assembled many years ago and frequently recounted. It is
because we know the continuity of a play like *Hamlet* that we

are able to experience it discontinuously. More important, by experiencing it discontinuously, we get to know it more intimately because its rhythms are closer to the ones that whip us through the Underground rush hour than the ones that nudged Shakespeare through the hills of Warwickshire. It is a trap to reiterate mindlessly that human nature remains fairly constant and that because the Elizabethan Age was one of expansion and exploration, and our own time is too, there is an inescapable similarity between the 1660s and the 1960s. There is – quite literally – a *world* of difference between the 1960s and the 1940s, between the 1950s and the 1930s, and, considering the frequency with which nations topple and thought transforms, next month may be the beginning of a completely new millennium, and this month we would not even have a hint of it. The two overriding contemporary facts are speed and change. We have always had change, but now that we have rapid, almost incessant change we must come to terms with the daily factor of speed: the relentless, insatiable motor-power that makes the world move as quickly as it does.

This, circuitously, brings me back to *Hamlet*. A collage technique is a way of transmitting speed in the theatre. It is a speed by which thoughts, actions, locales, and styles can be quickly shuffled. It has nothing to do with *pace*, the mechanical acceleration of Aristotle's 'slow-time'. Its speed is the result of being in many different places in quick succession and without predictable order. Some of these 'places' in *Hamlet* are:

The court at Elsinore
A plateau in the super-ego
The past as distorted by the present
The present as distorted by the past
A circus
An intellectual plane where various pieces of Shakespearian
    criticism commingle

Limbo
Heaven
Hell
A theatre.

SHORT BACKGROUND

This collage has had a chequered history. It started as a 28-minute condensation of *Hamlet* as part of the Theatre of Cruelty season at the LAMDA Theatre directed by Peter Brook and myself. There it was taken to be a 'clever exercise' and, in fact, was little more than that. But the problem it threw up made it difficult for me to leave it a Shakespearian charade. For the Festival of Experimental Theatres in Berlin, I enlarged the play to an hour and built in certain views I held about the character and 'notion' of *Hamlet*. In Berlin, the audience (mostly young people) gave it a four-minute standing ovation, but the critics roasted it. Frederick Luft, the leading German critic of *Die Welt*, was particularly vituperative. He flamed and fulminated against the ruination of Shakespeare, against Hamlet conceived 'as an ape of repressed action; an ape swinging from a rope'; was convinced it was a 'hoax' and concluded that, whatever it was, 'it leaves a bitter taste behind'. His notice triggered off a public demonstration at the Akademie der Künste, the theatre where it was performed, and leaflets attacking Luft's review were widely distributed. Luft answered the charges on German radio. A year later, now extended to its present length of an hour and a quarter, it was presented at the International Theatre Festival of Parma, where, again, the young members of the audience received it enthusiastically and the older members disparaged it. It then toured Italy, winding up in Rome, making friends and enemies in more or less equal amounts. In London, it was presented at the Jeanetta Cochrane Theatre, stirred up a cult following, but was largely ignored by the press and deemed a 'curiosity' by the one or two critics who saw it. The *Sunday Times* reviewer found it 'enthralling' and hoped the point of the exercise was to re-whet appetites for the wonders of the original – a notice which, from my viewpoint, succeeded in damning with loud praise. It has since been played in about twenty-five different countries, and reports have varied from 'unspeakably outrageous' to 'psychedelically uplifting'.

The Collage

*

CAST

HAMLET	CLOWN-POLONIUS*
FORTINBRAS	OPHELIA
GHOST	LAERTES
QUEEN	ROSENCRANTZ
KING	GUILDENSTERN

COURTIER (female)

* Polonius is played by the same actor as plays the clown, either by making a swift change in vocal characterization or, for example, by putting a grey-gloved hand to his chin to suggest a beard.

As presented by In-Stage for the Literarische Collo-
quium Berlin at the Akademie der Künste, 20 January
1965

HAMLET	Alexis Kanner
FORTINBRAS	Richard Poore
GHOST	John Citroen
QUEEN	Thelma Holt
KING	David Lloyd Meredith
CLOWN-POLONIUS	Anthony Hall
OPHELIA	Christine Curry
LAERTES	Laurie Asprey
ROSENCRANTZ	Robert Aldous
GUILDENSTERN	Roger Clayton
COURTIER	Linda Stockill

Designed by Tony Leah
Directed by Charles Marowitz

As presented by In-Stage throughout Italy and at the
Jeanetta Cochrane Theatre in London, 5 May 1966

HAMLET	Anthony Ainley
FORTINBRAS	Jonathan Newth
GHOST	John Citroen
GERTRUDE	Thelma Holt
CLAUDIUS	Richard Mayes
CLOWN-POLONIUS	Bill Wallis
OPHELIA	Christine Curry
LAERTES	Michael Jenkinson
ROSENCRANTZ	Jack Tweddle
GUILDENSTERN	Stuart Richmond
COURTIER	Gillian Watt

Designed by Ralph Koltai (London), Tony Leah (Italy)
Directed by Charles Marowitz

HAMLET *and* FORTINBRAS *stand facing each other. After a moment, Fortinbras moves down to meet the* CAPTAIN. *Hamlet falls in behind the Captain like a soldier in the ranks.*

FORTINBRAS:
Go, Captain, from me greet the Danish King.
Tell him, that by his licence Fortinbras
Craves the conveyance of a promis'd march
Over his kingdom.
HAMLET [*aside to Captain*]:
Good sir, whose powers are these?
CAPTAIN [*aside to Hamlet*]:
They are of Norway, sir.
FORTINBRAS:
You know the rendezvous.
HAMLET [*aside*]:
How purpos'd, sir, I pray you?
CAPTAIN [*aside*]:
Against some part of Poland.
FORTINBRAS:
If that his Majesty would aught with us,
We shall express our duty in his eye,
And let him know so.
CAPTAIN [*marching off*]:
I will do't, my Lord.
HAMLET:
Who commands them, sir?
CAPTAIN [*almost off-stage*]:
The nephew to old Norway, Fortinbras.

[HAMLET *moves downstage into a spot of his own.* FORTIN-
BRAS, *standing strongly behind him, slowly fades out.*]

HAMLET:

How all occasions do inform against me,
And spur my dull revenge. What is a man
If his chief good and market of his time
Be but to sleep and feed? A beast, no more:
Sure he that made us with such large discourse
Looking before and after, gave us not
That capability and god-like reason.

FORTINBRAS [*accusingly*]:

To rust in us unus'd.

GHOST:

If thou hast Nature in thee bear it not.
    [*Cut into new scene.*]

HAMLET:

Murder?

GHOST:

Murder most foul, as in the best it is;
But this most foul and unnatural.

HAMLET:

Haste, haste me to know it,
That I with wings as swift
As meditation or the thoughts of love
May sweep to my revenge.

QUEEN [*entering placating*]:

Come let me wipe thy face.

HAMLET [*to Ghost*]:

Speak, I am bound to hear.

OPHELIA [*entering*]:

You are keen, my Lord, you are keen.

QUEEN:

I prithee stay with us, go not to Wittenberg.

GHOST:

The serpent that did sting thy father's life . . .

QUEEN:

Do not forever with thy vailed lids
Seek for thy noble father in the dust.

GHOST:

Now wears his crown.

KING:

How is it the clouds still hang on you?

QUEEN:

Thou know'st 'tis common, all that lives must die . . .

GHOST:

By a brother's hand
Of life, of crown, and Queen at once dispatch'd.

QUEEN:

Passing through Nature, to Eternity.

HAMLET [*to Ghost*]:

Mine uncle?

GHOST:

Ay, that incestuous, that adulterate beast,
With witchcraft of his wits, with traitorous gifts
    won to his shameful lust
The will of my most seeming-virtuous Queen.

QUEEN:

Why seems it so particular with thee?

HAMLET [*to Queen*]:

Seems, Madam? nay, it is: I know not seems!
    [*The next two speeches are counterpointed with the King's in
    prominence, and the Ghost's as a dulled accompaniment.*]

KING:
'Tis sweet and commendable
  in your nature, Hamlet,
To give these mourning
  duties to your father.
But you must know, your
  father lost a father,
That father lost, lost his,
  and the survivor bound
In filial obligation for some
  term
To do obsequious sorrow.

GHOST:
With juice of cursed
  hebenon in a vial
...swift as quicksilver it
  courses through
The natural gates and
  alleys of the body;
And with a sudden vigour
  it doth posset
And curd, like eager
  droppings into milk,
The thin and wholesome
  blood ...

HAMLET [*to himself*]:
Hold my heart:
And you my sinews grow not instant old:
But bear me stiffly up.

KING:
Fie, 'tis a fault to Heaven,
A fault against the dead, a fault to Nature,
To reason most absurd whose common theme
Is death of fathers.

HAMLET:
If he but blench I know my course.

CLOWN [*suddenly appearing*]: What is he that builds stronger than either the mason, the shipwright or the carpenter?

HAMLET [*soberly to the King*]: The gallows-maker, for that frame outlives a thousand tenants.

CLOWN: I like thy wit well, in good faith, the gallows does well; but how does it well? It does well to those that do ill. To't again. Who builds stronger than a mason, a shipwright or a carpenter?

KING:
We pray you throw to earth

This unprevailing woe, and think of us
As of a father.

FORTINBRAS:
Think of us as of a father.

CLOWN:
Think of *us* as of a father.

QUEEN:
Thou has thy father much offended.

LAERTES:
And so have I a noble father lost.
    [*Coming out of Sound-Montage.*]

[*Sound-Montage:
all lines are
chanted and
overlap.*]

GHOST:
If thou didst ever thy dear father love ...

KING:
Remain
Here in the cheer and comfort of our eye,
Our chiefest courtier, cousin, and our son.

HAMLET:
O villain, villain, smiling damned villain!

KING:
Why 'tis a loving and a fair reply.

CLOWN [*coming in for tag-line*]: Cudgel thy brains no more
about it; say a grave-maker, the houses that he makes
last ...

GHOST:
Till the foul crimes done in my days of Nature
Are burnt and purged away.

CLOWN [*seeing Ghost – backing away*]:
How long will a man lie in the earth ere he rot?

GHOST [*to Hamlet*]:
By a brother's hand
Of life, of crown, and Queen at once dispatch'd.

HAMLET:
Mine uncle.

51

GHOST:

Cut off even in the blossoms of my sin,
Unhousel'd ...

HAMLET:

A murderer and a villain ...

GHOST:

Disappointed ...

HAMLET:

A slave ...

GHOST:

Unaneled ...

HAMLET:

A cutpurse of the empire and the rule ...

GHOST:

No reckoning made, but sent to my account
With all my imperfections on my head.

HAMLET:

A king of shreds and patches!

[*Cut into new scene.* KING *and* LAERTES *play oblivious of Hamlet.*]

LAERTES [*suddenly*]:

Where is my father?

KING:

Dead.

LAERTES:

I'll not be juggled with.
To hell allegiance; vows to the blackest devil.

HAMLET [*weakly trying to match Laertes' passion*]:

Yea, from the table of my memory
I'll wipe away all trivial fond records ...

LAERTES:

Conscience and grace to the profoundest pit.

HAMLET:

All saws of books, all forms, all pressures past.

LAERTES:
  I dare damnation.

HAMLET:
  I have sworn it.

LAERTES:
  ...to this point I stand,
  That both the worlds I give to negligence,
  Let come what comes: only I'll be revenged
  Most throughly for my father.

HAMLET:
  O thou vile King,
  Give me my father.

KING [*calming Laertes*]:
  Make choice of whom your wisest friends you will,
  And they shall hear and judge 'twixt you and me:
  If by direct or collateral hand
  They find us touch'd, we will our Kingdom give,
  Our Crown, our life, and all that we call ours
  To you in satisfaction.

HAMLET:
  So excellent a King that was to this Hyperion to a satyr.

KING [*turning on Hamlet, tauntingly*]:
  Was your father dear to you?
  Or are you like a painting of a sorrow,
  A face without a heart?

GHOST [*off-stage*]:
  Remember me!

HAMLET:
  O all you host of heaven. O earth what else?
  And shall I couple hell – Remember thee!
    [*Now swinging on rope which has suddenly appeared from above.*]
  Ay thou poor ghost; while memory holds a seat in this dis-
    tracted globe.
    [*Cut into Closet Scene.*]

QUEEN [*at right of Hamlet*]:

   This is the very coinage of your brain
   This bodiless creation ecstasy
   Is very cunning in.

HAMLET [*still on rope*]:

   Ecstasy?
   My pulse as yours doth temperately keep time
   And makes as healthful music. Mother, for love of Grace,
   Lay not a flattering unction to your soul
   That not your trespass but my madness speaks.
   Confess yourself to Heaven,
   Repent what's past, avoid what is to come,
   And do not spread the compost on the weeds
   To make them ranker. [*Coming off rope.*]
   I did love you once.

OPHELIA [*at left of Hamlet*]:

   Indeed my Lord, you made me believe so.

HAMLET:

   You should not have believed me. For virtue cannot so
   inoculate our old stock but we shall relish of it.

OPHELIA:

   I have remembrances of yours,
   That I have longed long to redeliver.
   I pray you now, receive them.

HAMLET:

   No, I never gave you aught.

OPHELIA:

   My honour'd Lord, you did,
   And with them words of so sweet breath compos'd
   As made the things more rich.

HAMLET [*to Ophelia*]:

   Are you honest?

QUEEN:

   O Hamlet, speak no more;

Thou turn'st mine eyes into my very soul,
And there I see such black and grained spots
As will not leave their tinct.

HAMLET [*to Ophelia*]:
Are you fair?

QUEEN:
These words like daggers enter in mine ears.

HAMLET:
Get thee to a nunnery. Why wouldst thou be a breeder of sinners?

CLOWN:
Cannot you tell that? every fool can tell that.

OPHELIA:
Thou hast cleft my heart in twain.

POLONIUS:
My Lord, the Queen would speak with you, and presently.

HAMLET:
Do you see that cloud that's almost in shape like a camel?

POLONIUS [*studying it*]:
By the mass, and it's like a camel indeed.

HAMLET:
Methinks it is like a weasel.

OPHELIA:
I was the more deceived.

HAMLET:
If thou dost marry, I'll give thee this plague for thy dowry. Be thou as chaste as ice, as pure as snow ...
   [*To Queen*]:
Go not to my uncle's bed,
Assume a virtue if you have it not!
   [*To Ophelia*]:

Thou shalt not escape calumny.

Get thee to a nunnery. Or if thou wilt needs marry, marry a fool: for wise men know what monsters you make of them.

POLONIUS [*still studying the cloud*]:

It *is* back'd like a weasel.

HAMLET:

Or like a whale?

POLONIUS:

Very like a whale.

HAMLET [*facetiously, of Polonius*]:

O what a noble mind is here o'erthrown.

[ROSENCRANTZ *and* GUILDENSTERN, *as vaudeville team, dance on. They are linked by a long rope that connects one to the other.*]

BOTH:

They bore him barefac'd on the bier,
Hey nonny, nonny, hey nonny, no.
And on his grave rain'd many a tear,
Hey nonny, nonny, no.

CLOWN [*pained by their performance*]:

The *time* is out of joint.

HAMLET:

Good lads, how do you both?

BOTH:

As the indifferent children of the earth.

ROSENCRANTZ:

Happy, in that

GUILDENSTERN:

We are not overhappy;

ROSENCRANTZ:

On Fortune's cap

GUILDENSTERN:

We are not the very button.

HAMLET:
Nor the soles of her shoe?

BOTH:
Neither, my Lord.

HAMLET:
Then you live about her waist, or in the middle of her favour?

BOTH [*clutching balls*]:
Her privates we. [*All yok it up.*]

HAMLET:
In the secret parts of Fortune: Oh, most true; she is a strumpet.
[*From opposite side a separate scene between* KING *and* ROSENCRANTZ *and* GUILDENSTERN.]

KING:
I entreat you both
That you vouchsafe your rest here in our Court
Some little time: so by your companies
To draw him on to pleasures, and to gather
So much as from occasions you may glean
That open'd lies within our remedy.

HAMLET [*in former scene*]: What have you, my good friend deserv'd at the hands of Fortune that she sends you to prison hither?

ROSENCRANTZ:
Prison, my Lord?

HAMLET:
Denmark's a prison.

QUEEN:
Your visitation shall receive such thanks
As fits a King's remembrance.
[*They are paid;* KING *and* QUEEN *exit.*]

ROSENCRANTZ:
We think not so, my Lord.

HAMLET: Why then 'tis none to you, for there is nothing either good or bad but thinking makes it so.

  [*All laugh.*]

CLOWN [*as referee*]: A hit, a hit, a palpable hit!

ROSENCRANTZ: Why then, your ambition makes it one; 'tis too narrow for your mind.

HAMLET: O God, I could be bounded in a nutshell and count myself a King of infinite space, were it not that I have bad dreams.

  [*All turn to Clown for judgement.*]

CLOWN: Nothing, neither way.

  [*Cut into new scene.*]

GUILDENSTERN [*secretively*]: Good my Lord.

HAMLET [*taken off to one side*]: What's the news?

GUILDENSTERN: Vouchsafe me a word with you.

HAMLET [*facetiously*]: Sir, a whole history.

GUILDENSTERN: The King, sir ...

HAMLET [*pleasantly*]: I know the King and Queen have sent for you.

GUILDENSTERN [*ignoring him*]: ... is in his retirement marvellously distempered.

HAMLET: With drink, sir.

  [*Mugs does a little dance-step.*]

GUILDENSTERN: Good my Lord, put your discourse into some frame, and start not so wildly from my affair.

HAMLET [*still clowning*]: I am tame, sir, pronounce.

GUILDENSTERN: My Lord, you once did love me.

HAMLET: Were you not sent for? Come, deal justly with me; nay speak.

ROSENCRANTZ: Good my Lord, what is your cause of distemper? You do surely bar the door of your own liberty, if you deny your griefs to your friend.

HAMLET: But to the purpose; what make you at Elsinore?

GUILDENSTERN: To visit you, my Lord. No other occasion.

[HAMLET *grabs them both by the neck.*]

HAMLET: Be even and direct with me, whether you were sent for or no.

GUILDENSTERN: What should we say, my Lord?

HAMLET: If you love me hold not off. [*Applies pressure.*]

ROSENCRANTZ [*gurgling*]: My Lord, we were sent for.

  [HAMLET *shoves them both away, towards the King, but still keeps a tight rein on them — literally, holds the rope to which both are attached.*]

KING:

  And can you by no drift of circumstance
  Get from him why he puts on this confusion,
  Grating so harshly all his days of quiet
  With turbulent and dangerous lunacy?

ROSENCRANTZ:

  He does confess he feels himself distracted,
  But from what cause he will by no means speak.

KING:

  Did he receive you well?

ROSENCRANTZ [*with a look back to Hamlet who holds his rein*]:
  Most like a gentleman.

  [HAMLET *yanks Rosencrantz's rope;* ROSENCRANTZ *is pulled back to Hamlet.*]

GUILDENSTERN:

  But with much forcing of his disposition.

  [HAMLET *yanks Guildenstern's rope, and he is pulled back to Hamlet. Hamlet unties them, pushes* ROSENCRANTZ *forward and out, and boots Guildenstern solidly on the rump.*]

GUILDENSTERN [*rubbing backside*]:

  Now cracks a noble heart.

  [*Exits.*]

  [*Cut into new scene.*]

QUEEN [*suddenly discovered*]:

  Why, how now Hamlet?

HAMLET [*of the booted-off Rosencrantz and Guildenstern*]:
   My excellent good friends,
   Whom I will trust as I will adders fang'd!
QUEEN:
   This is mere madness.
HAMLET:
   I must to England; you know that?
QUEEN:
   Nay then, I'll set those to you that can speak.
HAMLET:
   Do not come your tardy son to chide.
      [*Cut into school flashback.*]
QUEEN [*as teacher*]:
   Come, come and sit you down,
   And these few precepts in thy memory
   See thou character.
      [LAERTES, OPHELIA, *and the* CLOWN *sit down in a line in
      front of* HAMLET. *Teacher and class start beating out the
      iambic rhythm with their fingers against their palms, and the next
      is chanted out in a strictly scanned sing-song.*]
   Give thy thoughts ... [*points to Ophelia.*]
OPHELIA:
   No tongue.
QUEEN:
   Nor any unproportion'd thought his ... [*to Hamlet.*]
HAMLET:
   Act.
QUEEN:
   Be thou familiar but ...
CLOWN [*brightly, teacher's pet*]:
   By no means vulgar.
QUEEN [*to class*]:
   The friends thou hast, and their adoption tried,
   Grapple them to thy soul with hoops of steel.

But do not dull thy palm with entertainment
Of each unhatch'd, unfledg'd comrade.
   [*Scanning ends here.*]
Beware of entrance into a quarrel but being in
Bear it that the opposed may beware of thee.
Give every man thine ear, but ... [*to Laertes.*]

LAERTES [*after being coached by all*]:
  ... few thy voice.

QUEEN:
  Take each man's censure but ... [*to Ophelia.*]

OPHELIA:
  Reserve thy judgement. [*Slaps him without reason.*]

QUEEN:
  Costly thy habit as thy purse can buy
  But not express'd in fancy; rich not g—

CLOWN [*impetuously*]:
  Not gaudy!

QUEEN [*who had intended that one for herself*]:
  For the apparel oft proclaims the man.
  Neither a ... [*Cues each pupil accordingly.*]

HAMLET:
  Borrower

OPHELIA:
  Nor a

LAERTES:
  Lender ...

CLOWN:
  Be.

ALL [*skipping in a circle*]:
  For loan oft loses both itself and friend;
  And borrowing dulls the edge of husbandry.

QUEEN:
  This above all ...
    [*All stand formally in a line and recite in a childish sing-song.*]

ALL:

To thine own self be true,
And it must follow as the night the day
Thou canst not then be false to any man.

QUEEN [*after a teasing pause*]:

Farewell.

[*All dash out as if at the end of a school session, but* FORTINBRAS *catches Hamlet before he has a chance to go.*]

FORTINBRAS:

Come, come and sit you down;
You shall not budge

till I set you up a glass

Where you may see the inmost part of you.

[*On rostrum,* KING *and* GHOST *stand back to back as if discovered in a picture frame.*]

Look here upon this picture and on this –
The counterfeit presentment of two brothers.
See what a grace was seated on this brow:

GHOST [*of himself*]:

Hyperion's curls, the front of Jove himself,
An eye like Mars to threaten or command;
A station like the herald Mercury,
New-lighted on a heaven-kissing hill;

FORTINBRAS [*summing up*]:

A combination and a form indeed
Where every god did seem to set his seal
To give the world assurance of a man.

QUEEN [*from the side, as a starstruck teenager*]:

He was a man, take him for all in all
I shall not look upon his like again.

FORTINBRAS:

Look you now what follows:
A murderer and a villain;

A slave that is not twentieth part the tithe
Of your precedent Lord.

KING [*of himself*]:
A vice of kings,
A cutpurse of the empire and the rule
That from a shelf the precious diadem stole
And put it in his pocket.

[*The* QUEEN *is scooped up into the* KING'S *arms, and he
proceeds to kiss and undress her. The* GHOST *steps down from
the picture frame and directs the next to the embracing couple.*]

GHOST:
O Hamlet, what a falling-off was there,
From me, whose love was of that dignity
That it went hand in hand, even with the vow
I made to her in marriage: and to decline
Upon a wretch whose natural gifts were poor
To those of mine.
          O horrible, horrible, most horrible.
If thou hast nature in thee bear it not.

HAMLET [*trying not to see the King and Queen making love before
his eyes*]: I have of late, but wherefore I know not, lost all my
mirth, foregone all custom of exercise; and indeed it goes
so heavily with my disposition, that this goodly frame the
earth seems to me a sterile promontory; this most excellent
canopy the air, look you, this brave o'erhanging firmament,
this majestical roof fretted with golden fire:

[GHOST *and* FORTINBRAS, *disgusted with Hamlet, exit
consulting together.*]

Why, it appears no other thing to me than a foul and
pestilent congregation of vapours.

Man delights not me ...

OPHELIA [*trying to seduce Hamlet. Singing*]:
By Gis, and by Saint Charity,
Alack and fie for shame:

Young men will do't, if they come to't.
　By Cock they are to blame.
Quoth she, before you tumbled me,
　You promis'd me to wed.
So would I ha' done, by yonder sun,
　And thou hadst not come to my bed.

HAMLET [*unmoved by all advances*]:
　... no nor woman neither.
　　[GHOST *suddenly enters with his arm around* FORTINBRAS,
　　as if he were his son and confiding in him.]

GHOST [*colloquially*]:
　If thou didst ever thy dear father love
　Revenge his foul and most unnatural murder.

FORTINBRAS [*imitating Hamlet*]:
　Haste, haste me to know it
　That I with wings as swift ...

HAMLET [*seeing his place usurped by Fortinbras*]:
　As meditation or the thoughts of love
　May sweep to my revenge.
　　[*Repeating speech, both play child's game — fist over fist — to
　　win toy sword.* HAMLET *wins then leaps forward gallantly.*]

HAMLET [*centre stage; consciously performing*]:
　Rightly to be great
　Is not to stir without great argument.

CLOWN [*with script, like exasperated director*]:
　Speak the speech, I pray you, as I pronounced it to you,
　　trippingly on the tongue.

HAMLET:
　But greatly to find quarrel in a straw ...

CLOWN:
　Nor do not saw the air too much with your hand thus, but
　　use all gently.

HAMLET:
　... greatly to find quarrel in a straw,

When honour's at the stake.

CLOWN:

Be not too tame neither.

HAMLET [*fiercely*]:

How stand I then

That have a father kill'd, a mother stain'd ...

CLOWN:

Suit the action to the word, the word to the action.

HAMLET [*gesturing*]:

That have a father kill'd a mother stain'd,

Excitement of my reason and my blood

And let all sleep.

CLOWN [*now as Polonius*]:

Fore God, my Lord, well spoken with good accent and good discretion.

[HAMLET, *exhausted and humiliated, has sunk to the ground.* CLOWN *has gone. Enter* OPHELIA.]

OPHELIA [*mock concern*]:

The glass of fashion and the mould of form,

The observed of all observers, quite, quite down [*sighs*]

[*The following scene is played out against flicker-wheel effect — like an old-time silent film.* HAMLET *sits on floor, entranced by all he sees. Shortly the* CLOWN *joins him, and both watch the film.*]

KING [*suddenly embracing Ophelia*]:

There's matter in these sighs.

These profound heaves

You must translate: 'tis fit we understand them.

What is't, Ophelia?

OPHELIA [*modestly*]:

So please you, something touching the Lord Hamlet.

KING [*suddenly releasing her, jealously*]:

What is between you, give me up the truth.

OPHELIA:

He hath, my Lord, of late made many tenders
Of his affection for me.

KING:

You speak like a green girl
Unsifted in such perilous circumstance.
Do you believe his tenders, as you call them?

OPHELIA:

I do not know, my Lord, what I should think.

KING:

Think yourself a baby
That you have ta'en his tenders for true pay
Which are not sterling. Tender yourself more dearly.

OPHELIA:

My Lord, he hath importun'd me with love
In honourable fashion.

KING:

Ay, fashion you may call it; go to, go to.

OPHELIA:

And hath given countenance to his speech, my Lord,
With all the vows of Heaven.

KING:

Love, his affections do not that way tend.
Do not believe his vows; for they are brokers,
Not of that dye which their investments show,
But mere implorators of unholy suits,
Breathing like sanctified and pious bawds,
The better to beguile.
I would not, in plain terms, from this time forth,
Have you so slander any moment leisure
As to give words or talk with the Lord Hamlet;
Look to't, I charge you.

OPHELIA:

I shall obey, my Lord.

[*The* KING, *regretting his harshness, embraces her.*]

KING:

Pretty Ophelia.

[*They kiss – and the scene dissolves.*]

CLOWN [*as prompter*]:

A father kill'd ... a mother stain'd ...

[HAMLET, *still transfixed by the scene, does not stir.*
As the movie lights come on again, the QUEEN *is discovered in*
KING's *arms;* OPHELIA *has vanished.*]

QUEEN [*after kiss*]:

Since my dear soul was mistress of my choice
And could of men distinguish, her election
Hath seal'd thee for herself. For thou hast been
As one in suffering all, that suffers nothing.
A man that Fortune's buffets and rewards
Hath ta'en with equal thanks. And blest are those
Whose blood and judgement are so well commingled
That they are not a pipe for Fortune's finger
To sound what stop she please. Give me that man
That is not passion's slave, and I will wear him
In my heart's core, ay, in my heart of heart
As I do thee.

[*The* QUEEN *kisses* CLAUDIUS, *and the scene dissolves.*
When lights fade up, it is the GHOST *discovered in the* QUEEN's
arms. He sits wearily. HAMLET *and* CLOWN, *still engrossed*
by film, continue to gape.]

GHOST:

Faith I must leave thee, and shortly too.

QUEEN [*soothingly*]:

You are so sick of late,
So far from cheer, and from your former state
That I distrust you: yet though I distrust,
Discomfort you, my Lord, it nothing must.
For women's fear and love holds quantity

67

In neither aught or in extremity.
Now what my love is, proof hath made you know
And as my love is siz'd, my fear is so.

GHOST [*wearily*]:

My operant powers their functions leave to do:
And thou shalt live in this fair world behind,
Honour'd belov'd and haply, one as kind
For husband shalt thou ...

QUEEN:

O confound the rest:
Such love must needs be treason in my breast.
In second husband let me accurst,
None wed the second, but who kill'd the first.

GHOST:

I do believe you think what now you speak,
But what we do determine, oft we break.

QUEEN:

The instances that second marriage move
Are base respects of thrift, but none of love.
A second time, I kill my husband dead
When second husband kisses me in bed.

GHOST:

The world is not for aye, nor 'tis not strange
That even our loves should with our fortunes change.
The great man down, you mark his favourite flies,
The poor advanc'd makes friends of enemies.
But orderly to end where I begun,
Our wills and fates do so contrary run,
That our devices still are overthrown,
Our thoughts are ours, their ends none of our own.
So think thou wilt no second husband wed:
But die thy thoughts, when thy first Lord is dead.

QUEEN:

Nor earth to give me food, nor Heaven light,

Sport and repose lock from me day and night.
Each opposite that blanks the face of joy,
Meet what I would have well, and it destroy.
Both here, and hence, pursue me lasting strife,
If once a widow, ever I be wife.

CLOWN [*from floor*]:

Well spoken with good accent and good discretion.

    [HAMLET, *still transfixed, shushes the Clown.*]

GHOST [*lying down*]:

Sweet, leave me here awhile,
My spirits grow dull, and fain I would beguile
The tedious day with sleep.

QUEEN [*soothingly*]:

Sleep rock thy brain,
And never come mischance between us twain.

    [*When* GHOST *is asleep, the* KING, *as Murderer, suddenly
    appears beside the* QUEEN. *The Queen, no longer the loving wife,
    appears as Accomplice. They both stare down at the sleeping man,
    and then abruptly turn on Hamlet. The silent-screen convention
    is abruptly broken.* KING *and* QUEEN *bearing down on Hamlet.*]

QUEEN: Thoughts black,
KING: hands apt,
QUEEN: drugs fit,
KING: and time agreeing
QUEEN: Confederate season,
KING: else no creature seeing.

QUEEN [*with vial*]: With Hecat's ban thrice blasted, thrice
infected.

Thy natural magic and dire property

    [*The vial is forced into Hamlet's hands.*]

KING:

On wholesome life, usurp immediately.

    [KING *and* QUEEN *force a helpless* HAMLET *to pour poison
    into the ears of his sleeping father.*]

GHOST [*shrieking, rising up and speaking straight into Hamlet's face*]: If thou hast Nature in thee bear it not!

[*The shriek has suddenly dissolved the entire scene, and* HAMLET, *with all the apparitions fled, is left entirely alone. The* CLOWN *stealthily sneaks back.*]

CLOWN [*as prompter*]:

A father kill'd ... a mother stain'd ...

HAMLET [*dully*]:

A father kill'd ... a mother stain'd ...

CLOWN [*decides to prompt from other part of speech*]:

Bestial oblivion ...

HAMLET [*revved up again*]:

Now whether it be

Bestial oblivion or some craven scruple

Of thinking too precisely on the event,

[CLOWN *breathes sigh of relief and departs, thankful he's got the show on the road again.*]

HAMLET [*continues*]:

A thought which quarter'd hath but one part wisdom

And ever three parts coward, I do not know

Why yet I live to say 'This thing's to do'

Sith I have cause ...

FORTINBRAS [*urging*]:

... and will and strength and means ...

HAMLET [*limply*]: To do it.

FORTINBRAS:

'This thing's to do.' [*Hands him toy sword.*]

HAMLET:

Now might I do it pat.

[*The Court suddenly appears in an eighteenth-century elaborately ornamented theatre box. Applause. The* GHOST *as Player-King downstage giving his performance.*]

This play is the image of a murder done in Vienna: Gon-zago is the Duke's name, his wife, Baptista: you shall see

anon: 'tis a knavish piece of work, but what o' that? Your
Majesty and we that have free souls, it touches us not: let
the gall'd jade winch, our withers are unwrung.

KING [*in box*]:

What do you call the play?

HAMLET:

The Mouse-Trap.

[*The* GHOST, *playing as old-time tragedian (Player-King),
begins.*]

GHOST [*histrionically*]:

But soft, methinks I scent the morning's air:
Brief let me be: sleeping within my orchard,
My custom always in the afternoon,
Upon my secure hour ... [*Kneels down.*]

HAMLET:

Now he is praying,
And now I'll do it.
And so he goes to Heaven,
And so I am revenged. That would be scanned:
A villain kills my father, and for that
I his sole son do this same villain send
To heaven ...
Oh, this is hire and salary not revenge.

[CLAUDIUS *is suddenly discovered kneeling in Ghost's
position.*]

KING [*hamming*]:

What if this cursed hand
Were thicker than itself with brother's blood,
Is there not rain enough in the sweet heavens
To wash it white as snow?

HAMLET:

He took my father grossly full of bread
With all his crimes broad blown, as flush as May,
And how his audit stands who knows, save Heaven?

And am I then revenged,
To take him in the purging of his soul,
When he is fit and seasoned for his passage?
KING:
Whereto serves mercy
But to confront the visage of offence?
And what's in prayer but this twofold force,
To be forestalled ere we come to fall,
Or pardoned being down? Then I'll look up ...
My fault is past. But oh, what form of prayer
Can serve my turn?

[*The Court applauds the King's histrionics and rushes out of box
to congratulate him.*]

HAMLET [*appealing to audience*]:
Am I a coward?
Who calls me villain; breaks my pate across?
Plucks off my beard and blows it in my face?
Tweaks me by the nose; gives me the lie in the throat
As deep as to the lungs? Who does me this?
Ha why, I should take it; for it cannot be
But I am pigeon-liver'd and lack gall
To make oppression bitter or ere this
I should have fatted all the region kites
With this slave's offal, [*to King*] bloody, bawdy, villain.
KING [*as Player-King, apologizing for performance*]:
Forgive me my foul murder.
HAMLET [*faltering*]:
Remorseless, treacherous, lecherous, kindless villain.
KING [*as himself, kneels*]:
Oh my offence is rank, it smells to Heaven,
It hath the primal eldest curse upon it.
A brother's murder. Pray can I not,
Though inclination be as sharp as will,
My stronger guilt defeats my strong intent,

HAMLET:

And like a man to double business bound
I stand in pause where I shall first begin
And both neglect.

GHOST:

If thou ... hast ... nature ... in thee ... bear ... it not.

FORTINBRAS:

I with wings as swift
As meditation or the thoughts of love ...

HAMLET [*as if having been coached*]: may sweep to my ...

QUEEN [*seeing Hamlet with sword*]:

Help, help, hoa.

HAMLET:

O vengeance!

[*Stabs the King, who is kneeling before him. Blackout as his sword enters. Lights up. The KING still praying, unhurt. Repeated twice. On third stab, POLONIUS falls forward.*]

POLONIUS:

Oh, I am slain! [*Falls forward, dead.*]

[*All, crying like banshees, dash out leaving Hamlet, the dead Polonius, and the Queen, grief-stricken at the corpse.*]

HAMLET:

Dead for a ducat, dead.

[*Cut sharply into new scene.*]

OPHELIA:

You are merry, my Lord?

HAMLET:

Who I?

OPHELIA:

Ay, my Lord.

HAMLET: O God, your only jig-maker; what should a man do but be merry? For look you how cheerfully my mother looks, and my father died within's two hours.

QUEEN [*with Polonius's corpse*]:
  Oh me, what hast thou done?
HAMLET [*to Queen*]:
  Such an act
  That blurs the grace and blush of modesty,
  Calls virtue hypocrite, takes off the rose
  From the fair forehead of an innocent love
  And sets a blister there.
  Lady, shall I lie in your lap?
OPHELIA:
  No, my Lord.
HAMLET:
  I mean, my head upon your lap.
OPHELIA:
  Aye, my Lord.
HAMLET:
  Do you think I meant country matters?
OPHELIA:
  I think nothing, my Lord.
HAMLET:
  That's a fair thought to lie between maids' legs.
OPHELIA:
  What is, my Lord?
HAMLET:
  Nothing.
    [HAMLET *kisses her roughly and lays her down, then leaves;*
    OPHELIA, *now distracted, slowly recovers.*]
OPHELIA [*sings*]:
  How should I your true love know
    From another one?
  By his cockle hat and staff
    And his sandal shoon.
  He is dead and gone, Lady,

74

He is dead and gone,
At his head a grass-green turf
At his heels a stone.
And will he not come again?
And will he not come again?
No, no, he is dead,
Go to thy death-bed,
He never will come again.

[*Before Ophelia's plaintive song is finished the Gravedigger's merry one has already begun.*]

CLOWN [*as Gravedigger*]:

In youth when I did love, did love,
Methought it was very sweet,
To contract O the time for a my behove,
O methought there was nothing meet.

But Age with his stealing steps
Hath claw'd me in his clutch:
And hath shipped me until the land
As if I had never been such.

[*As* OPHELIA *wanders off aimlessly and the dead* POLONIUS *sings his song from the prone position,* HAMLET *and* LAERTES *suddenly appear from opposite sides, each brandishing a wooden toy sword. They clank swords together and then begin elaborate warming-up exercises, while the* KING, QUEEN, *and Court troop on and group themselves formally, awaiting the commencement of the duel.*]

HAMLET:

Come on, sir.

LAERTES:

Come, my Lord.

KING:

If Hamlet give the first or second hit,
Or quit in answer of the third exchange,

Let all the battlements their ordnance fire.
The King shall drink to Hamlet's better health,
And in the cup a union shall he throw
Richer than that, which four successive Kings
In Denmark's Crown have worn.

                              Come begin.
And you the judges bear a wary eye.
[*They duel mechanically, then stop.*]

LAERTES:

Too much of water has thou, poor Ophelia,
And therefore I forbid my tears.

[*The Court applaud enthusiastically.* LAERTES *acknowledges
with a bow. They duel again, then stop.*]

HAMLET [*trying his style*]:

Doubt thou, the stars are fire,
Doubt that the Sun doth move,
Doubt truth to be a liar
But never doubt, I love.

[*The Court boo and hiss his paltry effort.*]

LAERTES [*still duelling*]:

Both the worlds I give to negligence,
Let come what comes: only I'll be revenged
Most throughly for my father.

[*The Court cheer Laertes' poetry. The duel continues.*]

HAMLET [*limply competing*]:

The play's the thing
Wherein I'll catch the conscience of the King.

[*All boo and hiss Hamlet's lame reply.*]

LAERTES [*flamboyantly*]:

I have a speech of fire that fain would blaze.

[*All cheer wildly.*]

HAMLET [*desperately rattling them off*]:

O what a rogue and peasant slave am I,
O that this too too solid flesh would melt,

76

There's a divinity that shapes our ends,
Frailty thy name is woman – the rest is silence.
Judgement.

CLOWN [*grudgingly*]:
A hit, a very palpable hit.

> [FORTINBRAS, *all by himself, very slowly and deliberately applauds Hamlet as the Court stonily looks on.* HAMLET *draws more encouragement from this than, objectively, he should.* ROSENCRANTZ *and* GUILDENSTERN *come forward while* HAMLET *duels coolly with* LAERTES, *who, unlike Hamlet, is fencing laboriously.*]

ROSENCRANTZ:
What have you done, my Lord, with the dead body?

HAMLET:
Alas, poor Yorick.

GUILDENSTERN:
Where's Polonius?

HAMLET:
At supper.

GUILDENSTERN:
At supper? Where?

HAMLET: Not where he eats, but where he is eaten, a certain convocation of politic worms are e'en at him.

ROSENCRANTZ: My Lord, you must tell us where the body is, and go with us to the King.

HAMLET: The body is with the King, but the King is not with the body. The King is a thing –

GUILDENSTERN: A thing, my Lord?

HAMLET: ... of shreds and patches. Did you think I meant country matters? Another hit, what say you? [*Running Laertes through.*]

LAERTES [*dropping his sword*]:
A touch, a touch, I do confess.

ROSENCRANTZ and GUILDENSTERN:
Where is Polonius?

HAMLET: In heaven; send thither to see. If your messenger find him not there seek him in the other place yourself.

ROSENCRANTZ: O my Lord, if my duty be too bold, my love is too unmannerly.

HAMLET [*proffering sword as if it were a recorder*]: Will you play upon this pipe?

GUILDENSTERN: My Lord, I cannot.

HAMLET [*to Rosencrantz*]: I pray you.

ROSENCRANTZ: Believe me, I cannot.

HAMLET: I do beseech you.

GUILDENSTERN [*humouring him*]: I know no touch of it, my Lord.

HAMLET: 'Tis as easy as lying; govern these ventages with your finger and thumb, give it breath with your mouth, and it will discourse most eloquent music. Look you, these are the stops.

[*Waggles the point near Rosencrantz and Guildenstern; they look on frightened. He mimes playing the sword as if it were a pipe, then offers it to Rosencrantz and Guildenstern to play upon. They hesitate out of fear and confusion; then, to humour him, come forward to pick up the sword — at that moment, he grabs them both and threatens them with the toy, which has now become lethal.*]

GUILDENSTERN [*struggling free*]: Nay, good my Lord, this courtesy is not of the right breed.

HAMLET: Why look you now, how unworthy a thing you make of me: you would pluck out the heart of my mystery; you would sound me from my lowest note to the top of my compass. Why do you think I am easier to be played on than a pipe? Call me what instrument you will, though you can fret me, you cannot play upon me.

[HAMLET *does a wild step around* Rosencrantz *and* Guildenstern *and ends by stabbing them both with the toy sword. After
being stabbed, they consult each other, and decide to die, which
they do, quite falsely.*]

CLOWN:

A hit, a very palpable hit!

HAMLET [*now mad with power*]:

Come for the third, Laertes; you but dally.

I pray you, pass with your best violence,

I am afeared you make a wanton of me.

[*Exits brandishing sword, with Clown.*

Cut to Burial Scene.

All gathered around Ophelia's *tomb,* LAERTES *with the*
CLERGYMAN.]

LAERTES [*soberly*]:

What ceremony else?

DOCTOR:

Her obsequies have been as far enlarged

As we have warranty. Her death was doubtful,

And but that great command o'ersways the order,

She should in ground unsanctified have lodged

Till the last trumpet.

LAERTES:

Must there no more be done?

DOCTOR:

No more be done!

We should profane the service of the dead

To sing sage requiem and such rest to her

As to peace-parted souls.

LAERTES:

Lay her in the earth

And from her fair and unpolluted flesh

May violets spring.

[LAERTES *steps to grave with flowers;* OPHELIA *appears and*

*accepts them as a gift from her brother, who now appears
flirting with a strumpet.*]

LAERTES [*preoccupied with his tart*]:

My necessaries are embarked; farewell,
And sister, as the winds give benefit
And convoy is assistant, do not sleep
But let me hear from you.

OPHELIA [*at loom*]:

Do you doubt that?

LAERTES:

For Hamlet, and the trifling of his favours,
Hold it a fashion, and a toy in blood;
A violet in the youth of primy nature:
Forward, not permanent, sweet, not lasting,
The perfume and suppliance of a minute,
No more.

OPHELIA:

No more but so.

LAERTES:

Perhaps he loves you now,
And now no soil nor cautel does besmirch
The virtue of his will. But you must fear
His greatness weighed, his will is not his own.
Be wary then, best safety lies in fear.
[*Snuggles with tart.*]

OPHELIA:

I shall the effect of this good lesson keep
As watchman to my heart;
'Tis in my memory lock'd
And you yourself shall keep the key of it.

LAERTES [*back in former scene*]:

I tell thee, churlish priest,
A ministering angel shall my sister be
When thou liest howling.

Hold off the earth awhile,
Till I have caught her once more in mine arms:
   [*Leaps into grave. The funeral group suddenly freeze into a
   tableau.*]
Now pile your dust upon the quick and dead
Till of this flat a mountain you have made
To o'ertop old Pelion or the skyish head
Of blue Olympus.

HAMLET [*reappearing*]:
   What is he whose grief
   Bears such an emphasis? whose phrase of sorrow
   Conjures the wandering stars and makes them stand
   Like wonder-wounded hearers. This is I,
   Hamlet the Dane.

CLOWN [*as prompter*]: Speak the speech, I pray you, as I pronounced it to you, trippingly on the tongue.

HAMLET [*to Laertes*]: Woo't drink up eisel? eat a crocodile?
   I'll do't.

CLOWN [*whispering*]: Nor do not saw the air too much with
   your hand thus, but use all gently.

HAMLET:
   Dost thou come here to whine,
   To outface me with leaping in her grave?
   Be buried quick with her, and so will I.

CLOWN:
   Be not too tame neither.

HAMLET:
   And if thou prate of mountains let them throw
   Millions of acres on us.

CLOWN:
   Suit the action to the word, the word to the action.

HAMLET:
   Throw
   Millions of acres on us, till our ground

Singeing his pate against the burning zone
Make Ossa like a wart. Nay, and thou'lt mouth.
I'll rant as well as thou.

QUEEN:

Alas, how is't with you?
That you bend your eye on vacancy,
And with the incorporal air do hold discourse.
Whereon do you look?
   [*Funeral ceremony still frozen in tableau.*]

HAMLET [*looking toward funeral scene*]:

Do you see nothing there?

QUEEN:

Nothing at all, yet all that is I see.

HAMLET:

Nor did you nothing hear?

QUEEN:

No, nothing but ourselves.
   [*Pause.*]

HAMLET [*collapsing into Queen's lap*]:

Your noble son is mad.
   [*Tableau dissolves.*]

QUEEN [*the mum, consoling*]:

Hear Hamlet, take my napkin; rub thy brows.

HAMLET [*nestling in her bosom*]:

You must needs have heard how I am punished
With sore distraction. What I have done
That might your nature, honour and exception
Roughly awake, I here proclaim was madness.

QUEEN:

Come, let me wipe thy face.

HAMLET [*still nestling*]:

I lov'd Ophelia; forty thousand brothers
Could not with all their quantity of love
Make up my sum.

QUEEN [*rocking Hamlet like a babe*]:
   Hamlet, Hamlet ...
HAMLET [*suddenly up; facing Queen*]:
   Go not to my uncle's bed.
      [*Pause.*]
QUEEN:
   No more.
HAMLET [*still restrained*]:
   You cannot call it love; for at your age
   The hey-day in the blood is tame, it's humble,
   And waits upon the judgement.
QUEEN:
   Hamlet, speak no more.
HAMLET [*losing control*]:
   Nay, but to live
   In the rank sweat of an enseamed bed
   Stew'd in corruption; honeying and making love
   Over the nasty sty.
KING [*entering*]:
   Good Gertrude, set some watch over your son.
HAMLET [*pushing her away*]:
   O shame! Where is thy blush? Rebellious Hell
   If thou canst mutine in a matron's bones,
   To flaming youth, let virtue be as wax
   And melt in her own fire.
QUEEN:
   Why, how now Hamlet?
HAMLET [*as if there had been no outburst*]:
   What's the matter now?
QUEEN:
   Have you forgot me?
HAMLET [*to the King*]:
   No, by the rood;
   You are the Queen, your husband's brother's wife

But would you were not so.
You are my mother.

KING:

Thy loving father, Hamlet.

HAMLET:

Father and mother is man and wife; man and wife is
one flesh, and so my mother.

KING [*moving off*]:

He is far gone; far gone.

QUEEN:

O heavenly powers, restore him.

KING:

Mad as the seas and wind when both contend
Which is the mightier.

[KING *and* QUEEN, *shaking heads, move away.*]

HAMLET [*to audience*]:

I am mad but north-north-west; when the wind is
southerly, I know a hawk from a handsaw.

ALL:

Judgement! Judgement! Judgement!

[*A trial is swiftly arranged:* HAMLET *placed in the dock by*
FORTINBRAS, *who acts as counsel. The* KING *acts as Judge.
All are seated behind a long tribunal table.*]

QUEEN:

Hamlet, thou hast thy father much offended.

HAMLET:

Mother, you have my father much offended.

KING [*as Judge*]:

Come, come, you answer with an idle tongue.

HAMLET:

Go, go, you question with an idle tongue.

KING:

Ophelia, prithee speak.

OPHELIA [*soberly giving testimony*]:

My Lord, as I was sewing in my chamber,
Lord Hamlet with his doublet all unbrac'd,
No hat upon his head, his stockings foul'd
Ungarter'd and down-gyved to his ankle,
Pale as his shirt, his knees knocking each other,
And with a look so piteous in purport,
As if he had been loosed out of hell,
To speak of horrors, he comes before me.

FORTINBRAS [*explaining*]: Mad for thy love.

OPHELIA:

My Lord, I do not know.

KING:

What said he?

OPHELIA:

He took me by the wrist and held me hard;
Then goes he to the length of all his arm,
And with his other hand thus o'er his brow,
He falls to such perusal of my face
As he would draw it. Long stay'd he so.
At last, a little shaking of mine arm;
And thrice his head thus waving up and down,
He rais'd a sigh so piteous and profound
As it did seem to shatter all his bulk
And end his being. That done, he lets me go,
And with his head over his shoulder turn'd,
He seemed to find his way without his eyes
For out a doors he went without their help,
And to the last bended their light on me.

FORTINBRAS [*to Court*]:

This is the very ecstasy of love
Whose violent property fordoes itself,
And leads the will to desperate undertakings
As oft as any passion under Heaven
That does afflict our natures.

OPHELIA [*slowly turning mad*]: I hope all will be well. We must be patient, but I cannot choose but weep to think they should lay him in the cold ground: my brother shall know of it, and so I thank you for your good counsel. Come, my coach: good night Ladies, good night sweet Ladies, good night, good night.

    [*Exits as if in the seat of a coach and six.*]

LAERTES [*of Ophelia*]:

O treble woe,

Fall ten times treble on that cursed head

Whose wicked deed thy most ingenious sense

Depriv'd thee of.

    [*Makes for Hamlet.*]

HAMLET: Away thy hand!

KING:

Pluck them asunder.

FORTINBRAS [*aside, to Hamlet*]:

Good my Lord, be quiet.

    [*To Court*]

Was't Hamlet wrong'd Laertes? Never Hamlet.

If Hamlet from himself be ta'en away

And when he's not himself does wrong Laertes,

Then Hamlet does it not. Hamlet denies it.

Who does it then?

CLOWN [*impulsively*]:

His madness.

FORTINBRAS: If't be so, Hamlet is of the faction that is wrong'd. His madness is poor Hamlet's enemy.

CLOWN [*to others behind table*]: That he is mad, 'tis true; 'tis true, 'tis pity, and pity 'tis, 'tis true.

GUILDENSTERN:

My Lord, the Queen would speak.

QUEEN [*rising*]:

Hamlet in madness hath Polonius slain.

ALL [*suddenly thumping table*]: Vengeance!

QUEEN:
In his lawless fit,
Behind the arras, hearing something stir,
He whips out his rapier and cries, A rat, a rat,
And in this brainish apprehension kills
The unseen good old man.

[*The* CLOWN, *as Polonius, rises and bows his head. All at the table bow their heads in condolence.*]

KING:
It had been so with us had we been there.

FORTINBRAS: Of that I shall have also cause to speak,
Wherein . . .

QUEEN: His liberty is full of threats to all; To you yourself, to
us, to everyone.

[*All thump table vengefully, as before.*]

HAMLET: [*rising to defend himself; Fortinbras struggles to keep him seated.*]
Indeed my lord,
I am very proud, revengeful, ambitious, with more offences
at my beck than I have thoughts to put them in, imagination
to give them shape, or time to act them in. What should such
fellows as I do, crawling between heaven and earth. We
are arrant knaves all, believe none of us.

[*The Court bristles with contempt and all agitatedly consult the King. Fortinbras talks urgently to Hamlet and forces a paper into hands.*]

FORTINBRAS [*Trying to undo Hamlet's harm*]:
My lord, will the King hear this.

HAMLET [*Rises, under sufferance, and reads prepared statement*]:
This presence knows,
And you must needs have heard how I am punish'd
With sore distraction. What I have done
That might your nature, honour and exception

Roughly awake, I here proclaim was madness.
LAERTES: Madness!
And so have I a noble father lost,
A sister driven into desperate terms,
Whose worth (if praises may go back again)
Stood challenger on the mount of all the age
For her perfections. But my revenge will come.
HAMLET:
Hear you, sir:
What is the reason that you use me thus?
I lov'd you ever.
LAERTES [*bristling with anger*]:
You mock me, sir.
HAMLET:
Not by this hand.
LAERTES [*springing on Hamlet*]: The devil take your soul.
    [*Others part Laertes and Hamlet. General scuffle stopped suddenly by the* GHOST'S *entrance.*]
GHOST:
Mark me.
HAMLET:
Alas, poor ghost.
KING:
Speak.
HAMLET:
Do not come your tardy son to chide
That laps'd in time and passion lets go by
Th' important acting of your dread command.
KING:
I charge thee, speak.
GHOST [*directly to King*]:
In the corrupted currents of this world,
Offence's golden hand may shove by justice,
And oft 'tis seen the wicked prize itself

Buys out the Law; but 'tis not so above,
There is no shuffling, there the action lies
In his true nature, and we ourselves compell'd
Even to the teeth and forehead of our faults,
To give in evidence.

[*Suddenly turns to* HAMLET, *who averts his gaze.*]

HAMLET [*to himself*]: How all occasions do inform ...

GHOST:

Eyes without feeling, feeling without sight,
Ears without hands, or eyes, smelling, sans all
Or but a sickly part of one true sense
Could not so mope.

HAMLET [*swearing to himself*]:

Thy commandment all alone shall live ...

GHOST: Let ... not ... the royal bed ... of Denmark ...
be ... a Couch ... for luxury and damned ... incest.

HAMLET [*kneeling before Father*]:

Thy commandment all alone shall live,
Within the book and volume of my brain,
Unmix'd with baser matter; yes, yes, by Heaven.
I have sworn't.

QUEEN [*rising*]:

And thus awhile the fit will work on him:
Anon as patient as the female dove,
When that her golden couplets are disclosed,
His silence will sit drooping.

[*All rise for verdict.*]

KING:

Confine him.
Madness in great ones must not unwatch'd go.

[*As Court moves off in all directions,* HAMLET *tries to stop
them with the next speech.*]

HAMLET:

Let me speak to th' yet unknowing world,

How these things came about, So shall you hear
Of carnal, bloody and unnatural acts,
Of accidental judgements, casual slaughters,
Of deaths put on by cunning, and forc'd cause,
And in the upshot, purposes mistook,
Fall'n on the inventors' heads. All this can I
Truly deliver.

> [*By the time* HAMLET *has finished his speech, he is ranting to the empty air as the Court have all disappeared.* FORTINBRAS, *sitting alone, looks up at him. Hamlet sinks down exhausted at his side.*]

FORTINBRAS:
So oft it chances in particular men
That for some vicious mole of nature in them
As in their birth – wherein they are not guilty,
Since nature cannot choose his origin, –
By the o'ergrowth of some complexion,
Oft breaking down the pales and forts of reason;
Or by some habit that too much o'er-leavens
The form of plausive manners; that these men,
Carrying, I say, the stamp of one defect,
Being nature's livery or Fortune's star,
Their virtues else, be they as pure as grace,
As infinite as man may undergo,
Shall in the general censure take corruption
From that particular fault.

HAMLET [*as if not understanding the implication*]:
Does it not, think'st thee, stand me now upon?
He that hath kill'd my King, and whor'd my mother,
Popped in between th' election and my hopes,
Thrown out his angle for my proper life,
And with such cozenage: is't not perfect conscience,

To quit him with this arm? and is't not to be damn'd
To let this canker of our nature come
In further evil?

FORTINBRAS [*patronizing*]:
Ay, marry, is't.

HAMLET [*acting*]:
Now could I drink hot blood,
And do such bitter business as the day
Would quake to look on.

FORTINBRAS [*trying another tack*]:
Rightly to be great
Is not to stir without great argument
But greatly to find quarrel in a straw
When honour's at the stake.

HAMLET [*hearing it for the first time*]:
How stand I then,
That have a father kill'd, a mother stain'd,
Excitements of my reason and my blood,
And let all sleep.

FORTINBRAS [*urging direct action*]:
Then trip him that his heels may kick at Heaven
And that his soul may be as damn'd and black
As Hell, whereto it goes.
    [*Pause.*]

HAMLET:
No.
When he is drunk asleep, or in his rage,
Or in the incestuous pleasure of his bed . . .

FORTINBRAS [*he's heard it all before*]:
Ay sure, this is most brave.

HAMLET [*on the defensive*]:
The spirit that I have seen

91

May be the devil ... the devil hath power
To assume a pleasing shape.
　　[FORTINBRAS, *unmoved by this ruse, regards Hamlet knowingly.*]
Do not look upon me,
Lest with this piteous action you convert
My stern effects; then what I have to do
Will want true colour.

FORTINBRAS:
That we would do
We should do when we would; for this 'would' changes,
And hath abatements and delays, as many
As there are tongues, are hands, are accidents,
And this 'should' is like a spendthrift sigh
That hurts by easing.

HAMLET [*seeking escape hatch*]:
How all occasions ...

FORTINBRAS [*taking him by the shoulders*]:
What would you undertake
To show yourself your father's son in deed
More than in words?

HAMLET [*squirming*]:
I'll ... observe his looks; I'll ... tempt him to the quick,
I'll have grounds more relative than this.

FORTINBRAS [*washing his hands of him completely*]:
Thus conscience does make cowards of us all,
And thus the native hue of resolution
Is sicklied o'er with the pale cast of thought
And enterprises of great pith and moment
With this regard their currents turn awry
And lose the name of action. [*Exits.*]
　　[*Long pause.*]

HAMLET [*bid to audience*]:
Had *he* the motive and the cue for passion

That I have, he would drown the stage with tears
And cleave the general ear with horrid speech,
Make mad the guilty and appal the free,
Confound the ignorant and amaze indeed
The very faculty of eyes and ears.

Yet I

A dull and muddy-mettled rascal ...
Peak like ...
John a' Dreams ... and

can do nothing.

[*Before the end of this speech, the* GHOST *and all the other characters have walked on very slowly. They form a semi-circle around the bent figure of Hamlet. Eventually, the Ghost comes forward. He is holding Hamlet's toy sword.*]

GHOST [*mock frightened*]:
Angels and ministers of grace defend us:
Be thou a spirit of health, or a goblin damn'd,
Bring with thee airs from Heaven or blasts from Hell?
Be thy intents wicked or charitable,
Thou comest in such a questionable shape
That I will speak to thee. I'll call thee Hamlet.

[*Puts toy sword under Hamlet's arm, like a crutch. The Cast, now fully assembled, expresses its delight over the Ghost's send-up.*]

CLOWN [*acknowledging its wit*]:
A hit, a very palpable hit.

GHOST [*still playing it up like mad*]:
Speak, I am bound to hear.

[*A long pause, during which everyone's sarcastic laughter gradually mounts.*]

HAMLET [*weakly*]:
To be or not to be that is the question.
[*All laugh.*]

[*Weakly*] The play's the thing wherein I'll catch the conscience of the King.

[*All laugh again.*]

[*Vainly trying to find the right words*] There is something rotten in the state of Denmark.

[*The laughter sharply cuts out. A powerful, stark silence issues from everyone. No one moves. Slowly* HAMLET'S *frame begins to bend, gradually his knees sag and his back arches until he slumps down on to his knees. Then his head slowly rolls forward on to his chest and he sinks even further, on to his haunches. He leans on his toy sword for support. This descent takes a good deal of time, and occurs in total silence.*]

FORTINBRAS [*coming out of semi-circle; sarcastically*]:

What a piece of work is man.

[*Chants*]

How noble in reason.

ALL [*chanting*]:

Noble in reason.

FORTINBRAS [*chants*]:

How infinite in faculty.

ALL [*chanting*]:

Infinite in faculty.

FORTINBRAS [*chanting*]:

In form and moving, how express and admirable.

ALL [*chanting*]:

Express and admirable.

FORTINBRAS [*chanting*]:

In action, how like an angel.

ALL [*chanting*]:

How like an angel.

FORTINBRAS [*chanting*]:

In apprehension, how like a god.

ALL [*chanting*]:

How like a god.

[*After this choral send-up led by* FORTINBRAS, *all look again to* HAMLET, *who has not stirred.*]

OPHELIA [*like old-time tragedienne, dashing forward.*]

O what a noble mind is here o'erthrown.

ALL [*Make a cry of being aghast.*]

OPHELIA:

The courtier's, soldier's, scholar's eye, tongue, sword.

ALL [*Make a sound of great mock anguish.*]

OPHELIA:

The expectancy and rose of the fair State.

ALL [*Make a sound of mock pity.*]

OPHELIA:

And I of ladies most deject and wretched
That suck'd the honey of his music vows.

ALL [*Make a sound commiserating with the girl's wretchedness.*]

OPHELIA:

Now see that noble, and most sovereign reason,
Like sweet bells jangled out of tune, and harsh,
That unmatch'd form and feature of blown youth,
Blasted with ecstasy. O woe is me ...

ALL [*wailing*]:

Woe is meeeeee ...

OPHELIA:

T' have seen what I have seen,
    [*Looks disgustedly at the slouched Hamlet.*]
See what I see.
    [*There is another stony silence, during which all watch the motionless Hamlet.*]

GHOST [*coming forward; the father of old*]:

If ... thou ... hast ... Nature ... in ... thee ... bear ... it not!

HAMLET [*still slumped; making a vow*]:

Thy commandment all alone shall live
Within the book and volume of my brain.

GHOST:
  Swear.
HAMLET:
  All saws of books ...
GHOST:
  Swear ...
HAMLET:
  All forms ...
GHOST:
  Swear.
HAMLET:
  All pressures past ...
GHOST:
  Swear!
HAMLET [*rising*]:
  Thy commandment all alone shall live.
    [*As he has struggled to his feet,* ROSENCRANTZ *and* GUIL-
    DENSTERN *come up to him – and at that moment, he collapses
    into their arms and is borne – like a dead soldier – to the
    pedestal.*]
FORTINBRAS:
  Bear Hamlet like a soldier to the stage
  For he was likely (had he been put on)
  To have prov'd most royally.
    [HAMLET, *slumped on circular pedestal, summons up one last
    burst of energy.*]
HAMLET:
  O Vengeance!
    [*Thrusts his toy sword into a host of imaginary victims. After
    each thrust, a character falls to the ground, truly slain, until the
    corpses of all the characters lie strewn around Hamlet like a set of
    downed ninepins.*]
  From ... this ... time ... forth
    [*The corpses, still stretched out, begin derisive laughter.*]

My thoughts be bloody or be nothing worth.
   [*Corpses, laughing hysterically, mock Hamlet with jeers, whistles, stamping and catcalls till final fade out.*]

CURTAIN

The Tragical History of
Dr Faustus

*

INTRODUCTION

It was while searching for a viable version of Marlowe's play for the Citizens' Theatre in Glasgow that I gradually came to realize that not only was FAUSTUS a flawed masterpiece but the enormity of those flaws almost invalidated the qualities which made it a masterpiece at all. The commonplace about the play, that it is half-a-dozen chunks of magnificent poetry interspersed with drivel and high-jinks, is a judgement I continually returned to no matter which version I read. One adaptor solved the problem of the inept comedy by cutting out all the scenes that interfered with Faustus' wails of conscience thereby converting the play into a turgid little sermon on good and evil the likes of which would have made the staunchest Christian scarper from the parish. Truncating an already-truncated work is obviously no answer, but neither can one proceed with odd fragments of an uneven play assuring oneself that if one simply 'plays Marlowe' all will be well. My ultimate conclusion is that there is no play at all – only a small wad of diffuse material most of which is thought to be Marlowe's, some of which is most certainly not Marlowe's and a good deal of which is clearly the work of hacks so inferior to Marlowe that it is criminal they should ever have horned in on the collaboration.

From a contemporary standpoint, the play's undercurrent, the assaulted conscience of a scientist who trespassed the bounds of permissible knowledge, has an almost exact parallel in the case of J. Roberts Oppenheimer and certain other nuclear physicists who first enthused and then abominated the making of the atom and hydrogen bombs. The problem was to try to insinuate that parallel without upsetting the specifics of Marlowe's Christian parable. In the Glasgow production, the mixture was uneven, and the Oppenheimer subtext too brashly indicated in superficies. In the Frankfurt production at the Festival of Experimental Theatre, the problem was still not completely solved. At the Folkteatern in Göteborg, I decided to be as explicit as possible using filmed excerpts from contemporary texts and direct allusion. I incorporated topical elements of satire and a modernity of behaviour that deliberately put a strain on the verse. There was a certain theatrical tang in mixing two antithetical styles, but no real resolution. No matter how pointed the 20th century references may be, the 17th century parable always has the last word. My current feeling is that the play should be forsaken and a completely new work created which would use only the *gest* of the original but none of its language.

For the Swedish production, to help pave the way for the contemporary implications, I wrote a short dialogue between Faustus and Oppenheimer which I include here. If the ideas juggled in this chat could be assimilated in a production of the play, the work might be salvageable. Otherwise one must approach it as an invitation either to rhetoric or spectacle (or both) which, in my opinion, projects the play inspite of rather than because of its peculiar genius.

For the record: this version is based on the 1604 and 1616 editions of the play. It incorporates material from *Tamburlaine the Great* and the *Faustbuch* from which it is believed Marlowe derived his original play. I have taken a few liberties with structure; dumped a few characters and invented a few others.

CONVERSATION IN PURGATORY

FAUSTUS:

I've looked forward to this chat for quite some time Julius. May I call you Julius?

OPPENHEIMER:

Please do. I rarely used the name in my lifetime and made a point of not doing so at my hearing, but I'm quite reconciled to it now.

FAUSTUS:

Good. The first question I want to put to you is this: Now that it's all over with and all the scandal has died down, – was it worth it?

OPPENHEIMER:

Do you mean would I do it again?

FAUSTUS:

Yes, I suppose that is what I mean.

OPPENHEIMER:

I'm not hedging Doctor but frankly, that is exactly the question I wanted to put to you. May I?

FAUSTUS:

By all means. The answer is certainly I would. A scientist – a true scientist that is – has no choice. He is always peeking into the future like some helpless voyeur who cannot resist the next titillation. Even if I was assured that perpetual damnation lay in store for me, still I would not be able to act other than I did.

OPPENHEIMER:

I'm relieved to hear you say that because I would have answered in exactly the same way. It's easy for moralists to hand down judgements after the event, but when they need us – when they are desperate for our brains – the moral issues are never raised. I was told the Germans were working on the atom-bomb. The future of mankind depended on our side perfecting it first. When we discovered it was all a fiction – that the Germans knew next to nothing about atomic energy – I was told we must continue in any case as they may soon discover the formulae and we

must beat them to the punch. When the terrible thing
actually exploded and the concept of radioactive death was
revealed, I tried to dissuade them from the hydrogen
project. But then it was the Russians we were supposed to
beat . . . and so it went on until the horrors lay
stockpiled all over the world. By ourselves we
scientists are quite helpless and, in fact, harmless. It is
only when the bloody governments take us over that we
become lethal.

FAUSTUS:

You needn't tell me Julius. I had my share of all that
'national glory' business. Do you think Truman or
Eisenhower were any different from Carolus the Fifth?
Like all puffed-up national leaders, they feed on the
prestige of their scientists. Of course, they maligned me
afterward, a good man gone wrong and all that, but when
divinity and physics lead one logically to necromancy,
what is one to do? One cannot be crucified for pursuing
logic.

OPPENHEIMER:

Precisely. Relativity and the discovery of the neutron
brought us – logically – to atomic weaponry. Should one
abandon relativity and nuclear science because in certain
hands they can produce destruction? One may as well
abandon fire because it sometimes leads to arson.

FAUSTUS:

Although I agree with you in principle Doctor, let us be
candid with one another. There is a difference you must
admit, between a few conjuring-tricks and full-scale
global decimation. I may have consorted with the devil,
but you actually manufactured his goods.

OPPENHEIMER:

I beg to disagree Doctor. Your sin was by far the greater
because you established the precedent that scientific

inquiry should have no limits. The very existence of
scientists like myself stems from the fact that you
obliterated the line that marked off the permissible bounds
of knowledge. In one sense, dear Doctor, it is you and not
I who are the Father of the Atom Bomb.

FAUSTUS:

But in my day knowledge was severely limited. It was
before Edison, before the steam-engine, before the
Age of Reason. Scientifically speaking, it was the dark ages.

OPPENHEIMER:

But that darkness suited most people. They didn't crave
any brighter light. When you brought it, it was the
equivalent of my nuclear explosion. Your discovery
threatened Christianity with diabolism, the supremacy of
Good with the triumph of Evil. My experiments threaten
the continuance of life as we know it. It seems to me our
crimes are entirely equal. If anything, yours is the greater
as it preceded mine by five centuries thereby making
mine possible.

FAUSTUS:

You have a jesuitical turn-of-mind Julius. The last time I
heard such arguments they were being expounded by
Lucifer's bright-eyed boy.

OPPENHEIMER:

Be that as it may: I cannot accept the hypothesis that I
deserve damnation more than you.

FAUSTUS:

But I was a man alone. My actions affected only me. Surely
your responsibility was greater.

OPPENHEIMER:

During those terrible, conscience-ridden fifties,
everyone was bleating about 'responsibility'. The word
has lost whatever meaning it may have had. In the final
analysis, responsibility belongs to the people who pay for

it. When I was in Gottingen in the Twenties, my responsibility was to science – pure and simple. I was my own master and my hypotheses served as stimulating after-dinner chat and little else. During the war, my 'responsibility' was hired by the government. I was a man in the ranks just like the lowliest infantryman and, like him, I had to take orders and serve the common good. When I realized the full consequences of the Manhattan Project and what hydrogen energy could release, I felt it my duty to point this out to my superiors. And for this, I was removed from my position and publicly dishonoured. That doesn't bother me – although it did at the time. What does annoy me is that people can talk of 'my responsibility' without including their own. The tax-payer, then as now, is responsible for the manufacture of nuclear war-heads and chemical gases. The British are responsible for the American armaments race because they do not oppose American policy. The Swedes are responsible for nuclear proliferation because while they adopt superior moral postures, their economy is geared to help in the production of essential materials. You, Doctor Faustus, can you tell me – where was your responsibility?

FAUSTUS:

To my intellect. Ultimately, a man is responsible only for himself; *his* thoughts and *his* actions. He cannot be held responsible for the whole world. I cannot be held responsible if Carolus appropriates my ingenuity for political ends. That is Carolus's responsibility and if his people support him, *their* responsibility. The ultimate responsibility is with those who wield power; not with their underlings.

OPPENHEIMER:

My point exactly. One is responsible to oneself, or to others as they purchase one's time and talent. One

cannot go on being responsible for all mankind. Surely
that is what God is for.

FAUSTUS:

Precisely, and since He doesn't exist, where does that leave
us?

OPPENHEIMER:

In precisely the dilemma we have always been – where the
notion of responsibility is used as a stick to beat those whose
actions we may dislike.

FAUSTUS:

As for myself, I had a responsibility to my intelligence
which could not be shirked. That is why I was obliged to
study black magic.

OPPENHEIMER:

As for *my*self, I had a responsibility to all the scientific
research that preceded me. I had to make the 'next step'
or the whole idea of scientific progress would have been
repudiated.

FAUSTUS:

Most people, you know, cannot understand scientific
principles.

OPPENHEIMER:

True, but then most people are so pathetically
unscientific, Doctor.

FAUSTUS:

Too true, too true. But let me ask you this Julius:
Do you think there is any useful purpose being served by
our damnation? I mean, would you say it acted as an
effective deterrent?

OPPENHEIMER:

My dear Doctor, as you implied earlier, there is
no such thing as a deterrent where the human mind is
concerned. I understand that in England and America at
the moment, there are giant factories where our

colleagues are perfecting discoveries that make our achievements look puny indeed. In Porton, they have the bubonic plague in bottles. At the Dow Chemical Works in America, they have perfected a bomb that totally consumes human life but safeguards property.

FAUSTUS:

Really, I wonder what sort of formula that is based on.

OPPENHEIMER:

A quite simple one. Would you like me to explain the principle?

FAUSTUS:

I should be delighted if you could spare the time ...

OPPENHEIMER:

Time is what we both have in abundance, Doctor. It's quite simple really. Just imagine, if you will, the flame of a candle magnified 150 million times. ...

[*The two scientists move off, disputing.*]

The Adaptation

*

CAST

DR FAUSTUS
JUDGE
FIRST MONK
SECOND MONK
THIRD MONK
FOURTH MONK
FIFTH MONK
PROSECUTOR
WAGNER
GOOD ANGEL
EVIL ANGEL
VALDES
CORNELIUS
FIRST SCHOLAR
SECOND SCHOLAR
THIRD SCHOLAR
MEPHISTOPHILIS
EMPEROR
EMPRESS
KNIGHT
ALEXANDER
PARAMOUR
CLOWN
POPE
ARCHBISHOP
FRIARS

LUCIFER
DIPLOMAT
PRIDE
COVETOUSNESS
WRATH
ENVY
GLUTTONY
SLOTH
LECHERY
CARTER
COURSER
DICK
ROBIN
DUKE
HELEN
FIRST COURTIER
SECOND COURTIER
SERVANT
COURT
CARDINALS
CROWD
GERMANY
FRANCE
AMERICA
ENGLAND

Scene: Lights come up on DR FAUSTUS *sitting on stool, tense, expectant. Nothing happens. After a moment, a group of hooded* MONKS *file in very quickly and take up positions behind a long rectangular table, which is so arranged as to suggest trial proceedings. They stand waiting. The* JUDGE-*figure, dressed identical to Dr Faustus, enters and takes up position at the head of table. Judge gives a signal; all sit, except him.*

JUDGE:

Though thou hast now offended like a man,
Do not persever in it like a devil.
O gentle Faustus, leave this damned art,
This magic, that will charm thy soul to Hell
And quite bereave thee of salvation.
Yet, yet, thou hast an amiable soul,
If sin by custom grow not into nature.
Then, Faustus, will repentance come too late;
Then thou art banish'd from the sight of Heaven;
No mortal can express the pains of Hell.
It may be this my exhortation
Seems harsh and all unpleasant; let it not,
For, gentle son, I speak it not in wrath
Or envy of thee, but in tender love
And pity of thy future misery;
And so have hope that this my kind rebuke,
Checking thy body, may amend thy soul.
   [*Pause.*
   FAUSTUS *looks up fearfully.*]
FIRST MONK:
   O my dear Faustus, what imports this fear?

SECOND MONK:

What ails Faustus?

THIRD MONK [*to Second*]:

He is not well with being over-solitary.

SECOND MONK:

If it be so, we'll have physicians and Faustus shall be cured.

THIRD MONK:

'Tis but a surfeit, sir, fear nothing.

JUDGE:

A surfeit of deadly sin that hath damned both body and soul.

SECOND MONK:

Yet, Faustus, look up to Heaven and remember God's mercy is infinite.

PROSECUTOR [*coming forward, dossier in hand, to begin his case*]:

Faustus' offence can ne'er be pardoned. The serpent that tempted Eve may be saved, but not Faustus. Gentlemen, hear me with patience and tremble not at my speeches, as I recount

[*Opening dossier*]

The tragical history of Dr Faustus.

[*To audience as to members of a jury*]

Not marching in the fields of Trasimene,

Where Mars did mate the warlike Carthagens;

Nor sporting in the dalliance of love,

In courts of kings where state is overturn'd;

Nor in the pomp of proud audacious deeds

Intends our Muse to vaunt his heavenly verse:

Only this, gentles – we must now perform

The form of Faustus' fortunes, good or bad:

And now to patient judgements we appeal,

And speak for Faustus in his infancy.

Now is he born, his parents base of stock,

In Germany, within a town call'd Rhodes;

At riper years to Wittenberg he went,
Whereas his kinsmen chiefly brought him up.
So much he profits in divinity,
The fruitful plot of scholarism grac'd,
That shortly he was grac'd with doctor's name,
Excelling all, and sweetly can dispute
In th' heavenly matters of Theology;
Till, swollen with cunning, of a self-conceit,
His waxen wings did mount above his reach,
And, melting, heavens conspir'd his overthrow;
For, falling to a devlish exercise,
And glutted now with learning's golden gifts,
He surfeits upon cursed necromancy;
Nothing so sweet as magic is to him,
Which he prefers before his chiefest bliss.

[*Cut to Faustus's study.* DOCTOR FAUSTUS *seated with* SCHOLARS. WAGNER, *wearing a laboratory apron, enters.*]

FAUSTUS:
Wagner, commend me to my dearest friends,
The German Valdes and Cornelius;
Request them earnestly to visit me.

WAGNER:
I will, sir.

FAUSTUS [*to himself*]:
Their conference will be a greater help to me
Than all my labours, plod I ne'er so fast.

[SCHOLARS *rise.* FAUSTUS *bids them good night. They go out.* FAUSTUS *takes out book from under desk and begins to peruse it.*]

GOOD ANGEL [*from his seat in the audience*]:
O Faustus, lay that damned book aside,
And gaze not on it lest it tempt thy soul
And heap God's heavy wrath upon thy head.
Read, read the Scriptures; that is blasphemy.

EVIL ANGEL [*from her seat in the audience*]:
Go forward, Faustus, in that famous art
Wherein all Nature's treasure is contain'd:
Be thou on earth as Jove is in the sky,
Lord and commander of these elements.

FAUSTUS:
How am I glutted with conceit of this!
Shall I make spirits fetch me what I please,
Resolve me of all ambiguities,
Perform what desperate enterprise I will?
I'll have them fly to India for gold,
Ransack the ocean for orient pearl,
And search all corners of the new-found world
For pleasant fruits and princely delicates;
I'll have them read me strange philosophy,
And tell the secrets of all foreign kings;
I'll have them wall all Germany with brass,
And make swift Rhine circle fair Wittenberg;
I'll levy soldiers with the coin they bring
And chase the Prince of Parma from our land
And reign sole king of all our provinces;
Yea, stranger engines for the brunt of war
Than was the fiery keel at Antwerp's bridge
I'll make my servile spirits to invent.

[VALDES *and* CORNELIUS *enter. They are middle-aged and Germanic-looking, and carry briefcases.* WAGNER *lingers on until* FAUSTUS *gives him a stern look, and then he exits.*]

Come, German Valdes and Cornelius,
And make me blest with your sage conference.
Know that your words have won me at the last
To practise magic and concealed arts;
Yet not your words only, but mine own fantasy,
That will receive no object, for my head

But ruminates on necromantic skill.
Philosophy is odious and obscure,
Both law and physic are for petty wits,
Divinity is basest of the three,
Unpleasant, harsh, contemptible, and vile;
Then, gentle friends, aid me in this attempt;
And I, that have with concise syllogisms
Gravell'd the pastors of the German church,
And made the flowering pride of Wittenberg
Swarm to my problems, as the infernal spirits
On sweet Musaeus when he came to hell,
Will be as cunning as Agrippa was,
Whose shadows made all Europe honour him.

VALDES:
Faustus,
These books, thy wit, and our experience
Shall make all nations to canonize us.

CORNELIUS:
As Indian Moors obey their Spanish lords,
So shall the spirits of every element
Be always serviceable to us three.

VALDES:
Like lions shall they guard us when we please,
Like Almain rutters with their horsemen's staves
Or Lapland giants trotting by our sides.

CORNELIUS:
Sometimes like women, or unwedded maids,
Shadowing more beauty in their airy brows
Than has the white breasts of the Queen of Love.

VALDES:
From Venice shall they drag huge argosies,
And from America, the golden fleece
That yearly stuffs old Philip's treasury,
If learned Faustus will be resolute.

FAUSTUS:

Valdes, as resolute am I in this
As thou to live: therefore object it not.

CORNELIUS:

The miracles that magic will perform
Will make thee vow to study nothing else.
He that is grounded in Astrology,
Enrich'd with tongues, well seen in minerals,
Hath all the principles magic doth require;
Then doubt not, Faustus, but to be renown'd
And more frequented for this mystery
Than heretofore the Delphian oracle.
The spirits tell me they can dry the sea
And fetch the treasure of all foreign lands,
Ay, all the wealth that our forefathers hid
Within the massy entrails of the earth.
Then tell me, Faustus, what shall we three want?

FAUSTUS:

Nothing, Cornelius. Oh, this cheers my soul!
Come, show me some demonstrations magical,
That I may conjure in some lusty grove
And have these joys in full possession.

VALDES:

Then haste thee to some solitary grove,
And bear wise Bacon's and Albanus' works,
The Hebrew Psalter, and New Testament,
And whatsoever else is requisite
We will inform thee ere our conference cease.

[CORNELIUS and VALDES *slowly place a hand on each of Faustus's shoulders and simultaneously repeat their speeches, backing out as they do so.* FAUSTUS, *drunk on their words, launches into his next speech before their voices have entirely faded.*]

FAUSTUS:

Oh, what a world of profit and delight,

Of power, of honour, of omnipotence
Is promis'd to the studious artisan!
All things that move between the quiet poles
Shall be at my command: emperors and kings
Are but obey'd in their several provinces,
Nor can they raise the wind or rend the clouds;
But his dominion that exceeds in this
Stretcheth as far as doth the mind of man;
A sound magician is a demi-god.

[*Cut back to Tribunal.* FAUSTUS, *once again, on his stool.*]

PROSECUTOR:

Yet art thou but still Faustus and a man.

[*Turning to those at table*]

If we say that we have no sin
We deceive ourselves, and there is no truth in us.
Why then, belike, we must sin
And so consequently die:

[*To Faustus*]

Ay, we must die an everlasting death.

[*Two* SCHOLARS *come before Faustus, still seated in his trial seat. They play out the following scene as if he were not there. Faustus watches it from the outside.*]

FIRST SCHOLAR:

I wonder what's became of Faustus, that was wont to make our schools ring with *sic probo*.

SECOND SCHOLAR:

He is within at dinner with Valdes and Cornelius.

FIRST SCHOLAR:

Then I fear he has fallen into that damned art for which those two are famous throughout the world.

SECOND SCHOLAR:

Were he a stranger and not allied to me, yet should I grieve for him. Come, let us go and inform the Rector, and see if he by his grave counsel can reclaim him.

FIRST SCHOLAR:

I fear me nothing can reclaim him.

[*Scholars' Scene dissolves as* PROSECUTOR *continues his brief.*]

PROSECUTOR:

Now that the gloomy shadow of the earth
Longing to view Orion's drizzling look,
Leaps from th'Antarctic world unto the sky
And dims the welkin with her pitchy breath,
Faustus, begin thine incantations,
And try if devils will obey thy hest,
Seeing thou hast pray'd and sacrific'd to them.

[*Cut to Faustus's laboratory, with test-tubes, chemicals, chart of elements, etc.*]

FAUSTUS:

Within this circle is Jehovah's name
Forward and backward anagrammatiz'd,
The breviated names of holy saints,
Figures of every adjunct to the heavens,
And characters of signs and erring stars,
By which the spirits are enforc'd to rise:
Then fear not, Faustus, to be resolute
And try the uttermost magic can perform.

Now may all the gods of Acheron be favourable to me. Dash down the triply deity of God. [*Bangs table.*] Ye spirits of air and fire, of water, earth and sky, Prince of them all – great Lucifer, monarch of Burning Hell – I call upon you now . . . let Mephistophilis rise. [*Stands up.*] Why do you wait? Why do you wait? By God and hell and all the fiends therein; by holy water, which I sprinkle, by the cross on which I trample, send great Mephistophilis himself to come and do me service.

[*Explosion. Faustus's face is disfigured by a psychedelic slide. Recoiling*]

I charge thee to return and change thy shape;

Thou art too ugly to attend on me.
[*Slide fades out.*]
I see there's virtue in my heavenly words.
Who would not be proficient in this art?
How pliant is Mephistophilis,
Full of obedience and humility!
Such is the force of magic and my spells.
Now, Faustus, thou art conjuror laureate,
That canst command great Mephistophilis.

[MEPHISTOPHILIS *dressed nattily in an expensive Italian suit, appears. His cuff-links glisten. His shoes have a high polish. He carries a briefcase.*]

MEPHISTOPHILIS:
Now, Faustus, what wouldst thou have me do?

FAUSTUS:
I charge thee wait upon me whilst I live,
To do whatever Faustus shall command,
Be it to make the moon drop from her sphere
Or the ocean to overwhelm the world.

MEPHISTOPHILIS:
I am a servant to great Lucifer
And may not follow thee without his leave;
No more than he commands must we perform.

FAUSTUS:
Did not he charge thee to appear to me?

MEPHISTOPHILIS:
I came hither of mine own accord.

FAUSTUS:
Did not my conjuring speeches raise thee? Speak.

MEPHISTOPHILIS:
That was the cause, yet only incidentally;
For when we hear one rack the name of God,
Abjure the scriptures and his saviour Christ,
We fly, in hope to get his glorious soul;

Nor will we come unless he use such means
Whereby he is in danger to be damn'd.
Therefore the shortest cut for conjuring
Is stoutly to abjure the Trinity
And pray devoutly to the prince of Hell.

FAUSTUS:

So Faustus hath
Already done, and holds this principle:
There is no chief but only Beelzebub,
To whom Faustus doth dedicate himself.
This word 'damnation' terrifies not him,
For he confounds hell in Elysium:
His ghost be with the old philosophers!
But leaving these vain trifles of men's souls,
Tell me, what is that Lucifer thy lord?

MEPHISTOPHILIS:

Arch-regent and commander of all spirits.

FAUSTUS:

Was not that Lucifer an angel once?

MEPHISTOPHILIS:

Yes, Faustus, and most dearly lov'd of God.

FAUSTUS:

How comes it then he is the prince of devils?

MEPHISTOPHILIS:

By aspiring pride and insolence,
For which God threw him from the face of heaven.

FAUSTUS:

And what are you that live with Lucifer?

MEPHISTOPHILIS:

Unhappy spirits that fell with Lucifer,
Conspir'd against our God with Lucifer
And are forever damn'd with Lucifer.

FAUSTUS:

Where are you damn'd?

MEPHISTOPHILIS:

In hell.

FAUSTUS:

How comes it then that thou art out of hell?

MEPHISTOPHILIS:

Why this is hell, nor am I out of it.
Think'st thou that I, who saw the face of God
And tasted the eternal joys of heaven,
Am not tormented with ten thousand hells
In being depriv'd of everlasting bliss?
O Faustus, leave these frivolous demands,
Which strike a terror to my fainting soul.

FAUSTUS:

What, is great Mephistophilis so passionate
For being deprived of the joys of heaven?
Learn thou of Faustus manly fortitude
And scorn those joys thou never shalt possess.
Go bear these tidings to great Lucifer:
Seeing Faustus hath incurr'd eternal death
By desperate thoughts against Jove's deity,
Say he surrenders up to him his soul
So he will spare him four and twenty years,
Letting him live in all voluptuousness,
Having thee ever to attend on me,
To give me whatsoever I demand,
To slay mine enemies and aid my friends,
To give me whatever I shall ask
To tell me whatsoever I demand,
And always be obedient to my will.
Go, and return to mighty Lucifer,
And meet me in my study at midnight
And then resolve me of thy master's mind.

MEPHISTOPHILIS:

I will, Faustus. [*Exit.*]

FAUSTUS:

Had I as many souls as there be stars,
I'd give them all for Mephistophilis.
By him I'll be great emperor of the world,
And make a bridge thorough the moving air
To pass the ocean with a band of men;
I'll join the hills that bind the Afric shore
And make that country continent to Spain,
And both contributory to my crown.
I'll burn the turrets of unruly towns
Flame, to the highest region of the air,
And kindle heaps of exhalations,
That being fiery meteors may presage
Death and destruction to the inhabitants:
Flying dragons, lightning, fearful thunderclaps,
Will singe the plains and make them seem as black
As the island where the Furies mask,
Compassed with Lethe, Styx and Phlegethon.
The Emperor shall not live but by my leave
Nor any potentate of Germany.

[*During Faustus's last lines, the Court of the Emperor has
slowly materialized. The* EMPEROR *is seated; beside him, the*
EMPRESS; *at his other side a surly* KNIGHT; *behind, the
members of the Court. The Emperor's greeting overlaps with the
end of Faustus's speech. When the scene is completely formed,*
FAUSTUS *steps into it.*]

EMPEROR:

Master Doctor Faustus, I have heard strange report of thy
knowledge in the black art, how that none in my Empire,
nor in the whole world, can compare with thee for the rare
effects of magic. They say thou hast a familiar spirit by
whom thou canst accomplish what thou list. This, therefore,
is my request, that thou let me see some proof of thy skill,

that mine eyes may be witnesses to confirm what mine ears have heard reported.

KNIGHT:

I' faith, he looks as like a conjuror as the Pope to a costermonger.

FAUSTUS:

My gracious sovereign, though I must confess myself far inferior to the report men have published, and nothing answerable to the honour of your imperial majesty, yet, for that love and duty binds me thereunto, I am content to do whatsoever your majesty shall command me.

EMPEROR:

Then, Doctor Faustus, mark what I shall say:
As I was sometime solitary set
Within my closet, sundry thoughts arose
About the honour of mine ancestors,
How they had won by prowess such exploits,
Got such riches, subdued so many kingdoms,
As we that do succeed, or they that shall
Hereafter possess our throne, shall,
I fear me, never attain to that degree
Of high renown and great authority;
Amongst which kings is Alexander the Great,
Chief spectacle of the world's pre-eminence,
The bright shining of whose glorious acts
Lightens the world with his reflecting beams,
As when I hear but motion made of him
It grieves my soul I never saw the man.
If, therefore, thou, by cunning of thine art,
Canst raise this man from hollow vaults below,
Where lies entomb'd this famous conqueror,
And bring with him his beauteous paramour,
Both in their right shapes, gesture and attire

They us'd to wear during their time of life,
Thou shalt both satisfy my just desire
And give me cause to praise thee whilst I live.

FAUSTUS:

My gracious Lord, I am ready to accomplish your request, so far forth as by art and power of my spirit I am able to perform.

KNIGHT:

An' your devils come not quickly, you shall have me asleep presently.

FAUSTUS:

But, if it like your grace, it is not in my ability to present before your eyes the true substantial bodies of those two deceased princes, which long since are consumed to dust.

KNIGHT:

Ay, marry, Master Doctor, now there's a sign of grace in you, when you will confess the truth.

FAUSTUS:

But such spirits as can lively resemble Alexander and his paramour shall appear before your grace in that manner that they both lived in, in their most flourishing estate; which I doubt not shall sufficiently content your imperial majesty.

EMPEROR:

Go to, Master Doctor, let me see them presently.

KNIGHT:

Do you hear, Master Doctor? Bring Alexander and his paramour before the Emperor!

FAUSTUS:

How then, sir?

KNIGHT:

And I'll be Actaeon and turn myself to a stag.

FAUSTUS:

And I'll play Diana and send you the horns presently.

KNIGHT:

Nay, an' you go to conjuring, I'll be gone. [*Exit.*]

FAUSTUS:

I'll meet with you anon for interrupting me so. – Here they are, my gracious lord.

[FAUSTUS *stands to one side, and* ALEXANDER *and his* PARAMOUR *appear in masks.*]

EMPEROR:

Sure, these are no spirits but the true substantial bodies of those two deceased princes.

[*Spirits exit.*]

FAUSTUS:

Will't please your highness now to send for the knight that was so pleasant with me here of late?

EMPEROR:

One of you call him forth.

[KNIGHT *enters, still facetious and aloof, but with horns on his head. The Court laughs uncontrollably.*]

FAUSTUS:

How now, sir Knight? I had thought thou hadst been a bachelor; but now I see thou hast a wife that not only gives thee horns but makes thee wear them.

[KNIGHT'S *aplomb withers as he notices everyone laughing at him and pointing to his head. He then puts his hands to his head and discovers the horns.*]

KNIGHT:

Thou damned wretch and execrable dog,
Bred in the concave of some monstrous rock,
How dar'st thou thus abuse a gentleman?
Villain, I say, undo what thou hast done!

FAUSTUS:

Are you remembered how you crossed me in my conference with the Emperor? I think I have met with you for it.

EMPEROR:

Good Master Doctor, at my entreaty release him. He hath
done penance sufficient.

FAUSTUS:

My gracious lord, not so much for the injury he offered me
here in your presence, as to delight you with some mirth,
hath Faustus worthily requited this injurious knight,
which, being all I desire, I am content to release him of his
horns: and, sir knight, hereafter speak well of scholars.

[*The Court, delighted with the show, applauds Faustus.*]

EMPEROR [*heard calling over applause*]:

Farewell, Master Doctor; yet, ere you go,
Expect from me a bounteous reward.

[*Cut back to Faustus in study.*]

FAUSTUS:

Come, Mephistophilis,
Now tell me what says Lucifer, thy Lord?

MEPHISTOPHILIS:

That I shall wait on Faustus whilst he lives,
So he will buy my service with his soul.

FAUSTUS:

Already Faustus hath hazarded that for thee.

MEPHISTOPHILIS:

But now thou must bequeath it solemnly
And write a deed of gift with thine own blood,
For that security craves Lucifer.
If thou deny it, I must back to hell.

FAUSTUS:

Stay Mephistophilis, and tell me what good
Will my soul do thy lord?

MEPHISTOPHILIS:

Enlarge his kingdom.

FAUSTUS:

Is that the reason why he tempts us thus?

MEPHISTOPHILIS:

'Misery loves company.'

FAUSTUS:

Why, have you any pain that torture others?

MEPHISTOPHILIS:

As great as have the human souls of men.
But tell me, Faustus, shall I have thy soul?
And I will be thy slave and wait on thee
And give thee more than thou hast wit to ask.

FAUSTUS:

Ay, Mephistophilis, I'll give it him.

MEPHISTOPHILIS:

Then, Faustus, stab thine arm courageously,
And bind thy soul, that at some certain day
Great Lucifer may claim it as his own;
And then be thou as great as Lucifer.

FAUSTUS:

Lo, Mephistophilis, for love of thee
Faustus hath cut his arm, and with his proper blood
Assures his soul to be great Lucifer's,
Chief lord and regent of perpetual night!
View here this blood that trickles from mine arm,
And let it be propitious for my wish.

MEPHISTOPHILIS [*with contracts*]:

But Faustus,
Write it in manner of a deed of gift.

FAUSTUS:

Ay, so I do. But, Mephistophilis,
My blood congeals, and I can write no more.

MEPHISTOPHILIS:

I'll fetch thee fire to dissolve it straight. [*Exits.*]

FAUSTUS:

What might the staying of my blood portend?
Is it unwilling I should write this bill?

Why streams it not, that I may write afresh?
Faustus gives to thee his soul: oh, there it stay'd!
Why shouldst thou not? Is not thy soul thine own?
Then write again, *Faustus gives to thee his soul.*

MEPHISTOPHILIS [*with cigarette-lighter*]:
See, Faustus, here is fire; set in on.

FAUSTUS:
So, now the blood begins to clear again;
Now will I make an end immediately.
It is done: this bill is ended,
And Faustus hath bequeathed his soul to Lucifer.
But what is this inscription on mine arm?
Homo, fuge: whither should I fly?
If unto God, he'll throw me down to hell.
My senses are deceiv'd; here's nothing writ:
Oh yes, I see it plain; even here is writ
Homo, fuge: yet shall not Faustus fly.

MEPHISTOPHILIS [*aside*]:
I'll fetch him somewhat to delight his mind.
See, Faustus, what our magic can perform
If learned Faustus will be resolute.

[*Sound of fireworks. Film of nuclear blasts.*]

FAUSTUS:
But may I raise such spirits when I please?

MEPHISTOPHILIS:
Ay, and do greater things than these.

FAUSTUS:
Then there's enough for a thousand souls.
Here, Mephistophilis, receive this scroll,
A deed of gift of body and of soul:
But yet conditionally that thou perform
All articles prescrib'd between us both.

MEPHISTOPHILIS:
Faustus, I swear by hell and Lucifer

To effect all promises between us made.

FAUSTUS:

Then hear me read it, Mephistophilis.

On these conditions following:

First, that Faustus may be a spirit in form and substance;

Secondly, that Mephistophilis shall be his servant and at his command;

Thirdly, that Mephistophilis shall do for him and bring him whatsoever;

Fourthly, that he shall be in his chamber or house invisible;

Lastly, that he shall appear to the said John Faustus at all times in what form or shape soever he please;

I, John Faustus of Wittenberg, Doctor by these presents, do give both body and soul to Lucifer, prince of the East, and his minister Mephistophilis.

MEPHISTOPHILIS:

And furthermore grant unto them that, four and twenty years being expired, the articles above-written inviolate, full power to fetch or carry the said John Faustus, body and soul, flesh, blood or goods, into their habitation wheresover.

Speak Faustus, do you deliver this as your deed?

FAUSTUS:

Ay, take it, and the devil give thee good on't!

MEPHISTOPHILIS [*placing it in briefcase, from which he takes whiskey flask and glass*]:

Now, Faustus, ask what thou wilt.

FAUSTUS:

First will I question thee about hell.

Tell me, where is the place that men call hell?

MEPHISTOPHILIS:

Under the heavens.

FAUSTUS:

Ay, so are all things else; but whereabouts?

MEPHISTOPHILIS:

Within the bowels of these elements,
Where we are tortur'd and remain forever.
Hell hath no limits, nor is circumscrib'd
In one self place, but where we are is hell,
And where hell is, there must we ever be;
And, to be brief, when all the world dissolves,
And every creature shall be purified,
All places shall be hell that is not heaven.

FAUSTUS:

I think hell's a fable.

MEPHISTOPHILIS:

Ay, think so still, till experience change thy mind.

FAUSTUS:

Why, dost thou think that Faustus shall be damn'd?

MEPHISTOPHILIS:

Ay, of necessity, for here's the scroll
In which thou hast given thy soul to Lucifer.

FAUSTUS:

Ay, and body too; but what of that?
Think'st thou that Faustus is so fond to imagine
That after this life there is any pain?
No, these are trifles and mere old wives' tales.

MEPHISTOPHILIS:

But I am an instance to prove the contrary,
For I tell thee I am damn'd and now in hell.

FAUSTUS:

Nay, and this be hell, I'll willingly be damn'd. What,
sleeping, eating, walking and disputing? ... But, leaving
this, let me have a wife, the fairest maid in Germany, for I
am wanton and cannot live without a wife.

MEPHISTOPHILIS:

I prithee, Faustus, talk not of a wife.
Marriage is but ceremonial toy;

And if thou lov'st me, think no more of it.
I'll cull thee out the fairest courtesans
And bring them every morning to thy bed;
She whom thine eye shall like, thy heart shall have,
Were she as chaste as was Penelope,
As wise as Sheba, or as beautiful
As was bright Lucifer before his fall.
Hold, take this book, peruse it thoroughly:
The iterating of these lines brings gold;
The framing of this circle on the ground
Brings thunder, whirlwinds, storm and lightning;
Pronounce this thrice devoutly to thyself
And men in harness shall appear to thee,
Ready to execute what thou command'st.

[FAUSTUS *takes up the book hungrily.*]

FAUSTUS:

Thanks, Mephistophilis; yet fain would I have a book wherein I might behold all spells and incantations, that I might raise up spirits when I please.

MEPHISTOPHILIS:

Here they are in this book. [*Proffers one.*]

FAUSTUS:

Now would I have a book where I might see all characters of planets of the heavens, that I might know their motions and dispositions.

[MEPHISTOPHILIS *passes over another book.*]

Nay let me have one book more, and then I have done, wherein I might see all plants, herbs, and trees that grow upon the earth.

[MEPHISTOPHILIS *hands over another.* FAUSTUS *begins to read them voraciously.*]

MEPHISTOPHILIS [*aside*]:

What will not I do to obtain his soul?

[*Fade out.*]

WAGNER [*with lab-apron*]:

Sirrah boy, come hither.

CLOWN:

How, boy! Swouns, boy, hast seen many boys with such whiskers as I have? [*Makes Wagner feel his non-existent beard.*]

WAGNER:

Tell me, boy, hast thou any comings in?

CLOWN:

Ay, and goings out too. You may see else. [*Protruding fingers from holes in pockets.*]

WAGNER:

Alas, poor slave, see how poverty jesteth in his nakedness; the villain is bare and out of service, and so hungry that I know he would give his soul to the devil for a shoulder of mutton, though 'twere blood-raw.

CLOWN:

Not so, good friend. I'd need have it well roasted and good sauce to it, if I pay so dear.

WAGNER:

Well, pock, wilt thou serve me, and I'll see that thou art not whipped more than twice each day?

CLOWN [*bowing and scraping*]:

O beneficient master; prithee I'll not harm thy broom-handle if thou'lt only deign to batter it about my head.

WAGNER:

Hold off, I say, and bind yourself to me, or I'll turn the lice about thee into familiars, and they shall tear thee to pieces.

CLOWN:

They are over-familiar with me already. Swounds, they are as bold with my flesh as if they had paid for their meat and drink.

WAGNER:

Well then, sirrah, come and take these guilders.

CLOWN [*wary*]:
And what should I do with these?

WAGNER:
Pocket them, I say.

CLOWN:
I trust not gifts from grasping friends.

WAGNER [*shoving them into his hands*]:
Now, sirrah, thou art at an hour's warning, whensoever and wheresoever the Devil shall fetch thee.

CLOWN:
No, no – take your guilders again.

WAGNER:
Truly, I'll have none of 'em.

CLOWN:
Bear witness, I gave them him.

WAGNER:
Bear witness, I gave them him again.
[*A chase, during which* WAGNER *continually loads off guilders on to Clown and* CLOWN *repeatedly pushes them back on to Wagner. Finally* WAGNER *shoves them into Clown's mouth and whacks him on the back, causing them to be swallowed.*]
Now I will cause two devils presently to fetch thee away – Baliol and Belcher.

CLOWN:
Let your Baliol and Belcher come here. I've a roaring way about me when I am put to, and neither man nor devil is safe when I'm in spleen.

WAGNER [*conjuring*]:
Baliol ... Belcher ...
[WAGNER *mimes prodding, pinching, eye gouging and biting.* CLOWN, *through some form of auto-suggestion, responds to every gesture with the appropriate physical reaction.*]

CLOWN:
Are they gone? A vengeance on 'em! I could have abided

the pinching he-devil, but the she-devil had pincers in her teeth.

WAGNER:

Well, sirrah, wilt thou follow me?

CLOWN:

But do you hear? If I should serve you, would you teach me to raise up Baliol and Belcher?

WAGNER:

I will teach thee to turn thyself into anything. To a dog ...

CLOWN:

Nay, and I'll be forever smellin' my own stool.

WAGNER:

Or a cat ...

CLOWN:

My nose a'leak with milk all day?

WAGNER:

Or a beady-eyed, fang-toothed, ring-tailed rat ...

CLOWN:

Nay and I'll scare myself out of my wits a-shavin' of a morning.

WAGNER:

Any form that thou doth wish shall be granted you.

CLOWN [*bright idea*]: Might I be a duke, or a count?

WAGNER:

Nay greater than either of these. A regent, a chancellor, a royal king. Swathed in velvet like a monarch's bed, with fifty swains to do thy bidding. Rich mutton for thy table, lakes of beer to waddle in, and young, perfumed paramours with whited breasts like creamy milk all full and flowing.

[CLOWN, *carried away, begins kissing Wagner, and is repulsed.*]
But first, swear thy allegiance and in solemn ceremony too.

[WAGNER *demonstrates the 'solemn ceremony' with elaborate Masonic hand-signals which the* CLOWN *tries (badly) to imitate. The ritual ends with Clown on stomach, eyes focused on Wagner's heel.*]

Henceforth call me Master Wagner, and let thy left eye be diametrically fixed upon my right heel. *Left* eye, varlet: *Right* heel, whey-face!

[CLOWN, *correcting his position, crawls off behind Wagner.*]

BLACKOUT

Lights up on Trial as before: MONKS *at table;* FAUSTUS *seated in his chair.* PROSECUTOR *addresses tribunal.*

PROSECUTOR:
Learned Faustus,
To know the secrets of astronomy,
Graven in the book of Jove's high firmament,
Did mount him up to scale Olympus' top,
Where, sitting in a chariot burning bright
Drawn by the strength of yoked dragons' necks,
He views the clouds, the planets, and the stars,
The tropics, zones and quarters of the sky,
From the bright circle of the horned moon
Even to the height of highest firmament
And, whirling round with this circumference
Within the concave compass of the pole,
From east to west his dragons swiftly glide
And in eight days did bring him home again.
Not long he stay'd within his quiet house
To rest his bones after his weary toil,
But new exploits do hale him out again,
And, mounted then upon a dragon's back,
That with his wings did part the subtle air,
He then hath gone to prove cosmography
That measures coasts and kingdoms of the earth,
Arriving thence upon the hills of Rome

To see the Pope and manner of his court
And take some part of holy Peter's feast,
The which that day was highly solemniz'd.
   [*Cut to private chamber of the Pope.* MEPHISTOPHILIS *is*
   lounging on a red-plush seat; FAUSTUS *is beside him.*]

FAUSTUS:
   But tell me now, what resting-place is this?
   Hast thou, as erst I did command,
   Conducted me within the walls of Rome?

MEPHISTOPHILIS:
   I have, my Faustus, and for proof thereof
   This is the goodly palace of the Pope,
   And 'cause we are no common guests
   I choose his privy chamber for our use.

FAUSTUS:
   Oh, I do long to see the monuments
   And situation of bright-splendent Rome.
   Come, therefore, let's away.

MEPHISTOPHILIS:
   Nay, stay, my Faustus; I know you'd see the Pope
   And take some part of holy Peter's feast,
   The which in state and high-solemnity
   This day is held through Rome and Italy.
      [*To him close*]
   And then devise what best contents thy mind
   By cunning in thine art to cross the Pope,
   Or dash the pride of this solemnity.

GOOD ANGEL:
   Never too late, if Faustus will repent.

MEPHISTOPHILIS:
   To make his monks and abbots stand like apes,
   And point like antics at his triple crown;

EVIL ANGEL:
   Too late.

136

MEPHISTOPHILIS:

To beat the beads about the friars' pates,

Or clap huge thorns upon the Cardinals' heads;

GOOD ANGEL:

Never too late.

MEPHISTOPHILIS:

Or any villainy thou canst devise.

And I'll perform it, Faustus.

[GOOD AND EVIL ANGELS *simultaneously repeat 'Never too Late' and 'Too Late' until* FAUSTUS *shuts out their voices.*]

EVIL ANGEL:

Too late.

FAUSTUS:

Sweet Mephistophilis, thou pleasest me.

Whilst I am here on earth let me be cloy'd

With all things that delight the heart of man.

My four and twenty years of liberty

I'll spend in pleasure and in dalliance,

That Faustus' name, whilst this bright frame doth stand,

May be admir'd through the furthest land.

MEPHISTOPHILIS:

'Tis well said, Faustus; come, then, stand by me,

And thou shalt see them come immediately.

[*Song off-stage.*]

FAUSTUS:

I am content to compass them some sport

And by their folly make us merriment.

But charm me, Mephistophilis, that I

May be invisible to do what I please

Unseen by any whilst I stay in Rome.

MEPHISTOPHILIS [*renders him invisible*]:

So Faustus; now

Do what thou wilt, thou shalt not be discerned.

[POPE *and* CARDINALS *enter for banquet.*]

POPE:

Lord Archbishop of Rheims, sit down with us.
[*All sit round a circular table.*]

ARCHBISHOP:

I thank your holiness.

POPE:

Lord Raymond, pray fall to: I am beholding
To the Bishop of Milan for this so rare a present.
[*It is snatched out of Pope's hands and sent flying.*
POPE *checks around him; all are busy chatting and eating. He
checks ceiling, decides not to make a fuss. Picks up second
chicken-leg, and it too flies out of his hand.*]

POPE [*rising*]:

How now. Who snatch'd the meat from me? Villains, why
speak you not?
[*There is an embarrassed silence.*]

CARDINAL [*to get over the moment*]:

Your holiness, here's a most dainty dish
Was sent from a Cardinal in France.
[*It too goes flying. This time all have seen it; all rise in con-
sternation.*]

POPE:

What lollards do attend our holiness
That we receive such great indignity?
Fetch me the wine.
[*It is passed along the table to Pope. As he reaches for it,*
FAUSTUS *takes it up slowly – all watch it rise into the air –
then it is poured over the Pope's head.*]

Ye lubbers, look about
And find the man that doth this villainy
Or by our sanctitude you shall die.

ARCHBISHOP:

Please it your holiness, I think it be

Some ghost crept out of purgatory, and now
Is come unto your holiness for his pardon.

POPE:

It may be so:
Go, then, command our priests to sing a dirge
To lay the fury of this same troublesome ghost.
    [*Crosses himself.*
    Pandemonium sets in as FRIARS *begin a dirge to banish spirit.*
    Food flies about. CARDINALS *step all over each other in*
    attempts to escape. Whirring noises like jet engines in back-
    ground. Dirge-singing throughout.]

FRIARS:

'Cursed be he that stole his Holiness' meat from the table!
Maledicat Dominus!
Cursed be he that struck his Holiness a blow on the face.
Maledicat Dominus!
Cursed be he that took Friar Sandelo a blow on the pate.
Maledicat Dominus!
Cursed be he that disturbeth our holy dirge.
Maledicat Dominus, [*etc.*]

    [FRIARS, MONKS, CARDINALS, *etc. all scramble out*
    dishevelled and panic-stricken, dropping their possessions as they
    go. FAUSTUS, *laughing with delight, remains, with Mephisto-*
    philis. As his enjoyment subsides, he spies a crucifix left by one
    of the fleeing monks. He gradually becomes sullen and quiet.]

FAUSTUS [*bitterly*]:

When I behold the heavens, then I repent
And curse thee, wicked Mephistophilis,
Because thou hast depriv'd me of those joys.

MEPHISTOPHILIS:

'Twas thine own seeking, Faustus; curse thyself.
But think'st thou heaven is such a glorious thing?
I tell thee, Faustus, it is not half so fair
As thou or any man that breathes on earth.

FAUSTUS:

How provest thou that?

MEPHISTOPHILIS:

'Twas made for man; then he's more excellent.

FAUSTUS:

If heaven was made for man, 'twas made for me:
I will renounce this magic and repent.

GOOD ANGEL:

Faustus, repent; yet God will pity thee.

EVIL ANGEL:

Thou art a spirit; God cannot pity thee.

FAUSTUS:

Who buzzeth in mine ears I am a spirit?
Be I a devil, yet God may pity me;
Yea, God will pity me if I repent.

EVIL ANGEL:

Ay, but Faustus never shall repent.

FAUSTUS:

Come, Mephistophilis, let us dispute again,
And reason of divine astrology.
Speak, are there many spheres above the moon?
Are all celestial bodies but one globe
As is the substance of this centric earth?

MEPHISTOPHILIS:

As are the elements, such are the heavens,
Even from the moon unto the empyreal orb,
Mutually folded in each other's spheres,
All jointly move upon one axle-tree,
Whose termine is term'd the world's wide pole.

FAUSTUS:

But have they all
One motion, both in position and in time?

MEPHISTOPHILIS:

All move from east to west in four and twenty hours upon

the poles of the world, but differ in their motion upon the
poles of the zodiac.

FAUSTUS:

These slender questions Wagner can decide;
Hath Mephistophilis no greater skill?
Who knows not the double motion of the planets?
These are freshmen's suppositions.
But tell me – who made the world?
   [*Mephistophilis does not reply.*]
I charge thee, tell me, who made the world?

MEPHISTOPHILIS:

I will not.

FAUSTUS:

Sweet Mephistophilis, tell me.

MEPHISTOPHILIS:

Move me not, Faustus.

FAUSTUS:

Villain, have not I bound thee to tell me anything?

MEPHISTOPHILIS:

Ay, that is not against our kingdom.
'This is. Thou art damn'd; think thou of hell.

GOOD ANGEL [*rising in his seat in auditorium*]:

Think, Faustus, upon God, that made the world.

MEPHISTOPHILIS [*to him*]:

Remember this. [*Exits.*]

FAUSTUS:

Ay, go, accursed spirit, to ugly hell!
'Tis thou hast damn'd distressed Faustus' soul.
Is't not too late?

EVIL ANGEL:

Too late.

GOOD ANGEL:

Never too late, if Faustus will repent.

EVIL ANGEL:

  If thou repent, devils shall tear thee in pieces.

GOOD ANGEL:

  Repent, and they shall never raze thy skin.

FAUSTUS:

  Oh, Christ, my saviour, my saviour,

  Help to save distressed Faustus' soul.

  [*Begins tearing up papers. Sudden sound of motors.* LUCIFER,
  *dressed in military garb, appears. With him, a soft, pudgy man
  who looks like a Tory diplomat.*]

LUCIFER:

  Christ cannot save thy soul, for he is just;

  There's none but I have interest in the same.

FAUSTUS:

  What art thou?

LUCIFER:

  I am Lucifer,

  And this, my companion prince in hell.

FAUSTUS:

  O Faustus, they are come to fetch thy soul.

DIPLOMAT:

  We come to tell thee thou dost injure us.

LUCIFER:

  Thou call'st on Christ, contrary to thy promise.

DIPLOMAT:

  Thou should'st not think on God.

FAUSTUS:

  Nor will I henceforth; pardon me in this,

  And Faustus vows never to look to heaven,

  Never to name God or to pray to him,

  To burn his scriptures, slay his ministers,

  And make my spirits pull his churches down.

LUCIFER:

  So shalt thou show thyself an obedient servant,

And we will highly gratify thee for it.

DIPLOMAT:

Faustus, we are come in person now to show thee some pastime. Sit down, and thou shalt see the Seven Deadly Sins appear to thee in their own proper shapes and likeness.

FAUSTUS:

That sight will be as pleasant to me as paradise was to Adam the first day of his creation.

DIPLOMAT:

Talk not of paradise or creation, but mark the show. Mephistophilis, fetch them in.

[DIPLOMAT *claps his hands, and the study is invaded by a horde of stamping, cheering rowdies – a group like a vulgar seaside audience bellowing for the show to begin. They beat the study table on which they sit.*]

LUCIFER:

Now, Faustus, question them of their names and dispositions.

FAUSTUS:

That shall I. What art thou, the first?

[*All the* SEVEN DEADLY SINS *are played by Mephistophilis, who wears six masks caricaturing different heads of state. The seventh, lechery, is depicted by a conventionally sexy female mask.*]

PRIDE:

I am Pride. I disdain to have any parents. I am like to Ovid's flea; I can creep into any corner of a wench; sometimes, like a periwig, I sit upon her brow; next, like a necklace, I hang about her throat; then, like a fan of feathers, I kiss her lips; indeed I do – what do I not? But fie, what a scent is here! I'll not speak another word, unless the ground be perfumed, and covered with cloth of arras.

FAUSTUS:

Thou art a proud knave, indeed.

[*The crowd hoots off Pride.*]

And what art thou, the second?

COVETOUSNESS:

I am covetousness, begotten of an old churl, in a leather
bag: and, might I have my wish, this place, and you and all,
should turn to gold, that I might lock you safe into my
chest. Oh, my sweet gold!

[*The crowd hoots off Covetousness.*]

FAUSTUS:

And what art thou, the third?

WRATH:

I am Wrath. I had neither father nor mother: I leapt out of
a lion's mouth when I was scarce an hour old; and ever
since I have run up and down the world with this case of
rapiers, wounding myself when I could get none to fight
withal. I was born in hell; and look to it, for some of you
shall be my father.

[*The crowd hoots off Wrath.*]

FAUSTUS:

What art thou, the fourth?

ENVY:

I am Envy, begotten of a chimney-sweeper and an oyster-
wife. I cannot read, and therefore wish all books were
burnt. I am lean with seeing others eat. Oh, that there
would come a famine over all the world, that all might
die, and I could live alone! Thou should'st see how fat
I'd be. But thou must sit, and I stand? Come down, with
a vengeance!

FAUSTUS:

Away, envious rascal.

[*The crowd hoots off Envy.*]

Now, what art thou, the fifth?

GLUTTONY:

Who, I, sir? I am Gluttony. My parents are all dead, and the
devil a penny they have left me, but a bare pension, and

that buys only ten meals a day – a small trifle to suffice nature. Oh, I come of a royal parentage; my father was a gammon of bacon, my mother a hogshead of claret-wine. Now Faustus, thou hast heard all my progeny; wilt thou bid me to supper?

FAUSTUS:

Not I, I'll see thee hanged first!

GLUTTONY:

Then the devil choke thee!

FAUSTUS:

Choke thyself, glutton!
[*The crowd hoots off Gluttony.*]
What art thou, the sixth?

SLOTH:

Heigh-ho, I am Sloth. I was begotten on a sunny bank where I have lain ever since, and you have done me great injury to bring me from thence. Heigh-ho, let me be carried there by Gluttony and Lechery. I'll not speak another word for a king's ransom.

FAUSTUS:

And what are you, Mistress Minx, the seventh and last?

LECHERY:

Who, I, sir? I am one that loves an inch of raw mutton better than an ell of fried stockfish; and the first letter of my name begins with L. [*Comes forward to Faustus.*] L . . . as in Lechery.

LUCIFER:

Enough . . . enough!
[*The Crowd and Seven Deadly Sins vanish as quickly as they arrived.*]

FAUSTUS:

Oh, how this sight doth delight my soul!

LUCIFER:

But Faustus, in hell is all manner of delight.

FAUSTUS:

Oh, might I see hell and return again safe, how happy were I then!

LUCIFER:

Faustus, thou shalt; at midnight I will send for thee. Meanwhile peruse this book and view it thoroughly, and thou shalt turn thyself into what shape thou wilt.

FAUSTUS [*fondling book*]:

Thanks, mighty Lucifer.

This will I keep as chary as my life.

[WAGNER *enters and nips book from under Faustus's arm.*]

WAGNER:

Oh, this is admirable! Here I ha' stolen one of Dr Faustus' conjuring books and, i'faith, I mean to search some circles for my own use. Now will I make all maidens in our parish dance at my pleasure stark naked before me, and so by that means I'll see more than e'er I saw yet.

CLOWN [*entering*]:

Ho, Master Wagner, I have searched far and wide for thee this morning.

WAGNER:

Keep out, goatshead! Keep out or else you are dismember'd, for I am about a roaring piece of work.

CLOWN:

What doest thou with that book? Canst thou read?

WAGNER:

Not all books are meant for reading, ox-brain.

CLOWN:

Why, what book is that?

WAGNER:

What book? Why, the most intolerable book for conjuring that e'er was invented by any brimstone devil.

CLOWN:

Canst thou conjure with it?

WAGNER:

I can do all things easily with it. I can make thee drunk with ippocras at any tavern in Europe; that's one of my conjuring works.

CLOWN:

I'faith, I can do that 'pon witchcraft of my own!

WAGNER:

Canst thou turn thyself into a flea?

CLOWN [*suddenly interested*]:

Canst thou do that for me?

WAGNER:

There is little within the poles I cannot accomplish with this.

CLOWN:

Oh, that would be well taken, sirrah. I have often wished to be as fleet as that agile insect; as tiny and as graceful.

WAGNER:

Prepare thyself then; I shall metamorphose thee.

CLOWN [*anxiously*]:

Wil'st truly? Oh, I flutter like a virgin on the brink.

WAGNER [*thumbing through pages*]:

'Tis writ in letters of red and black. Reincarnations. Fish, fowl, pheasant ... Fleas! The incantation is duly writ.

CLOWN [*tingling with anxiety*]:

Proceed, proceed ... and ere the day is out, I shall be whisking through the wench's plackets. Here, there, everywhere. I'll be amongst 'em i'faith.

WAGNER:

Art thou prepared for transformation?

CLOWN:

If I live to rival Solomon, I'll not readier be.

WAGNER:

I commence. [*Begins chanting.*]
Sanctobulorum Periphrasticon.

Sanctobulorum Periphrasticon.

Sanctobulorum Peri-phras-ti-con!

[*With last phrase,* WAGNER *opens his eyes to find* CLOWN *perched on box, eyes closed, ready to take flight.*]

Art thou a flea?

CLOWN:

Art thou an ass! Would a flea stand so waiting for a help-mate breeze to wing him on? O misery, methinks I shall never be a buzzing 'mongst the wenches.

WAGNER:

Thou needst be patient and resolute.

CLOWN:

And so I am, sirrah, but get on with't!

WAGNER:

I shall try a spell more potent still – that in its time hath turned great elephants to fleas. Art thou prepared?

CLOWN:

To leave the world and enter it again, but pray make haste.

WAGNER [*incanting*]:

Consecratum propitarius,

Consecratum propitarius.

Consecratum pro-pit-ar-i-us!

Thou art metamorphosed to a flea. Take wing.

[CLOWN *dives off box and lands heavily on stomach.*]

WAGNER [*irritably*]:

O hogshead, did'st ever see a flea fly so?

CLOWN [*licking bruises*]:

Nay, or hast thou seen a flea with both legs crippled to the bone, as this one is? Devil take your conjuring book and your brimstone duggery. I care not to be a flea. What, to become a smudge at a farmer's slightest itch; spend my days tickling pretty wenches and carrying it no further; set up house in a puppy's haunch? Fah, I'd as lief be an earth-worm and pass the hours chasing after my tail.

WAGNER [*flicking pages of book*]:
　Earthworm . . .

CLOWN:
　Swoun's, the villain hath me in the air or on the ground!
　'Tis best I quit him whilst I still can crawl. [*Begins crawling
　out.*]
　　[*Cut to Trial.*]

PROSECUTOR:
　When Faustus hath with pleasure ta'en the view
　Of rarest things, and royal courts of kings,
　He stay'd his course and so returned home,
　Where such as bare his absence with grief –
　I mean his friends and nearest companions –
　Did gratulate his safety with kind words,
　And in their conference of what befell,
　Touching his journey through the world and air,
　They put forth questions of astrology,
　Which Faustus answer'd with such learned skill
　As they admir'd and wonder'd at his wit.
　Now is his fame spread forth in every land:
　Amongst this throng the Emperor is one,
　Carolus the Fifth, at whose palace now
　Faustus is feasted 'mongst his noblemen.
　　[*Cut to Banquet. Guests chatting. At end of table the Judge sits
　　like an unbidden guest, visible only to Faustus.* EMPEROR *rises.
　　Conversation subsides.*]

EMPEROR [*to Faustus at his side; with toast*]:
　Wonder of men, renown'd magician,
　Thrice-learned Faustus, welcome to our court.
　These deeds of thine in rendering our state
　Free from our professed enemies
　Shall add more excellence unto thine art
　Than if by powerful necromantic spells
　Thou could'st command the world's obedience.

Forever be beloved of Carolus,
And honour'd of the German emperor.
[*The group applauds as* FAUSTUS *rises.*]

FAUSTUS:

These gracious words, most royal Carolus,
Shall make poor Faustus to his utmost power
Both love and serve the German emperor;
For proof whereof, if so your grace be pleased,
The Doctor stands prepar'd by power of art
To cast his magic charms, that shall pierce through
The ebon gates of ever-burning hell
And hale the stubborn furies from their caves
To compass whatsoe'er your grace commands.

EMPEROR [*raising cup*]:

Master Doctor Faustus,
  [*All rise for toast*]
Thou shalt command the state of Germany
And live belov'd of mighty Carolus.
  [*The Banquet group thump the table in a steady rhythm like
  applause. From the other side of the stage, a more rapid and
  nervous thumping is heard. After a few seconds, the Banquet
  fades, and the Tavern Scene lights up.*]

*The Tavern is being used as a secret-meeting place. Carter, a
woman, Dick, Robin and Courser and others crowd around the
table.*

CARTER:

Are we all met, then?

COURSER:

Aye, all that were called to meet.

CARTER:

Start you the proceedings as you are senior here.

COURSER:

Nay, I'll not begin, for though I recognize some offence here, it is not meet I should preside.

[*All grumble their disagreement.*]

CARTER:

Nay, you are aptest for that place, and all here say the same.

[*They agree.*]

COURSER:

Well, say on. I'll not begin.

ROBIN:

Nor is there so great a need for one to speak as the grievance is felt by all, and well do we know the cause of that grievance be that damned conjuror, Doctor Faustus.

[*Mutters of agreement.*]

DICK:

The city is not safe from him — nor will the kingdom be lest his devilry be stopped. On this very night he sits, as he is wont to do so oft, in the palace of Carolus stirring up contagion and plotting 'gainst the innocent.

ROBIN:

Last week, or so 'tis claimed, that same villain spying out a field of healthy harvest that circled round the city, grew so incensed with the sight of fruitful crops that he did hatch a devilish powder, so potent in its compound, that but a sniff would flatten out a thousand mile of verdant farmland. This, at stroke of midnight, he did scatter over all the field; and next morning, grey and rotten ashes lay where once all living things did bloom and sprout together.

CARTER:

Since Faustus hath come to conjure in the city, I've seen, with my own eyes, six babes brought into the world with cloven hoofs for feet, and spines all rounded like a toad's. That he is a black magician and by the devil tutored in's craft is not to be doubted.

ROBIN:

And have we not all – with our own eyes – seen him conversing with dead spirits, ancient shades whose whitened bones have slept this four score year beneath the soil?

DICK:

The fiend conspires daily with death, and will bring plague and pestilence in his wake.

COURSER:

And yet his power is not only with the netherworld. He has the ear of Carolus, and is honoured of the State. What can such as we do to dislodge him? Better leave what can't be mended.

DICK:

Aye, and have his spirits fetch us all away. Nay, he must be seized and scorched for his villainy lest hell itself do come to reign on earth.

COURSER:

If we dare to tamper with his power then damned we shall be – and more miserable then ever yet we have been.

DICK:

I say, if we rise up all the crafts and burghers will rise up as well. For every one with eyes doth know the menace of the man.

ROBIN:

Aye, our action will be taken for a sign, and God will help to scourge the devils he has raised.

COURSER:

But will God stay the troopers at his side?

ROBIN:

God will do all to bring the demon down.

CARTER:

Would you do the devil's work, and let such wickedness thrive? Then God pity your cowardice and damn your timidity!

DICK:

Has he not conjured me as well – for since he's loosed his spirits in the town, my children quake at every thunderstorm and fear the heavens themselves will topple into hell.

ROBIN:

Then let us not hesitate, but act e'en now as he pours his poison into the Emperor's ear. Are we then resolved?

CARTER:

Aye, resolve we all.

[*All rise in agreement.*]

ROBIN [*to Courser*]:

What say you then. Shall we act as one?

COURSER [*after a pause*]:

Aye! And dispatch him while the heat is in our blood!

[*They drink and rush out.*

Cut back to Banquet Scene, the guests now more relaxed and slightly high.]

DUKE [*sitting beside Emperor*]:

Master Doctor Faustus, since our conference about fair ladies, which was the beautifulest in all the world, we have determined with ourselves that Helen of Greece was the admirablest lady that ever lived; therefore, Master Doctor, if you will do us so much favour, as to let us see that peerless dame of Greece, we should think ourselves much beholding unto you.

FAUSTUS:

For that I know your friendship is unfeigned,
It is not Faustus' custom to deny
The just requests of those that wish him well.
You shall behold that peerless dame of Greece,
No otherwise for pomp or majesty
Than when Sir Paris cross'd the seas with her,
And brought the spoils to rich Dardania.
Be silent, then, for danger is in words.

[HELEN *in Grecian mask appears.*]

FIRST COURTIER:

Was this fair Helen, whose admired worth
Made Greece with ten years' war afflict poor Troy?
Too simple is my wit to tell her praise,
Whom all the world admires for majesty.

SECOND COURTIER:

No marvel though the angry Greeks pursued
With ten years' war the rape of such a queen,
Whose heavenly beauty passeth all compare.

EMPEROR:

Now we see the pride of Nature's work,
And only paragon of excellence.

[HELEN *exits.*]

Thanks, Master Doctor, for these pleasant sights,
As nothing in the world doth please me more.

FAUSTUS:

I am highly recompensed, my good lord, that it pleaseth
your highness. But gracious lady, it may be that you have
taken no pleasure in these sights; therefore, I pray you, tell
me, what is the thing you most desire to have? Be it in the
world, it shall be yours. I have heard that great-bellied
women do long for things that are rare and dainty.

[*The Court is amused.*]

EMPRESS:

True, Master Doctor, and since I find you so kind, I will
make known to you what my heart desires to have;
and were it now summer, as it is January, a dead time of
winter, I would request no better meat than a dish of ripe
grapes.

[*The Court laughs at her naïveté.*]

FAUSTUS:

This is but a small matter. Madam, I will do more than this
for your content.

[*The grapes suddenly drop from above and are handed to the Empress.*]

How now, taste ye these; they should be good, for they come from a far country, I can tell you.

EMPEROR:

This makes me wonder more than all the rest
That at this time of the year, when every tree
Is barren of his fruit, from whence you had
These ripe grapes.

EMPRESS:

And trust me, they are the sweetest grapes that e'er I tasted.
[*The grapes are doled out amongst much merriment. Suddenly there is a disturbance without. The group at table rise in agitation.*]

EMPEROR:

What rude disturbers have we at the gate?
Go, pacify their fury, set it ope,
And then demand of them what they would have.

SERVANT:

Why, how now, masters, what a coil is there?
What is the reason you disturb our court?
[*Hub-bub.*]

EMPEROR:

What would they have?

SERVANT:

They all cry out to speak to Doctor Faustus.

FAUSTUS:

I do beseech your grace, let them come in.
They shall be good subject for a merriment.

EMPEROR:

As thou wilt, I give thee leave, Faustus.

FAUSTUS:

I thank your grace.
[*The tavern-crowd scramble in on all sides of the banquet table,*

slightly uncertain of themselves at finding no barrier to their entry.]

Why, how now, my good friends –

Faith you are too outrageous; but come near, I have pro-cur'd your pardons: welcome all.

ROBIN:

'Tis your pardon thou shouldst procure – from Heaven, if thou hadst not been spurned from the face of it.

FAUSTUS:

How, spurned from Heaven? And who is your Good Intelligencer, pray?

DICK:

Our eyes. No other Intelligencer do we need.

FAUSTUS:

An' your eyes be your Intelligencer, they must needs send back opposite reports, so crossed be they in their sockets.

[The Court laughs.]

DICK:

I can see well enough a villain when there be one, and that sight is ungainly.

FAUSTUS:

If thou wouldst be spared it, when thou shavest of a morning, turn thy head in t'other direction.

[The Court laughs.]

CARTER:

The devil well knows how to scatter wit to trammel up the truth, but there are those throughout the town do know the evil that you wreak. Think not thy sins shall go unpunished.

FAUSTUS:

My sins? – and what be they?

ROBIN:

Your conjuring and your spells.

OTHER:

Your sins upon the land.

SECOND OTHER:

Your hexes on the newborn babes.

THIRD OTHER:

Your sorties with the dead.

FAUSTUS:

Why, what a busy conjuror is that who can raise spirits, smite forests and warp children – all in a trice. Art thou certain there are not three Faustuses – or twelve – or a score of them all conjuring at once throughout the cosmos.

CARTER:

An' if there be, we'll rout them out – each and everyone!

ROBIN:

And set them flaming on the stake.

FAUSTUS:

Ten thousand victims flaming on the stake! God wot, thou'lt make an Hades here on earth will be the envy of Prince Lucifer.

[*The Court laughs.*]

DICK:

He sports with us as if with spaniels at his feet.

FAUSTUS [*turning grim*]:

And are ye not? Nay, worse than spaniels? Curs and gutter-rats, lice and snails and carriers of plague. A gaggle of drab, bedraggled vermin!

[*All leap on Faustus, who charms them into contorted, paralysed poses. . . . The Court squeals with laughter as he changes their poses from one to another. Then, at a final click of his fingers, they all fall over and lie still. The laughter of the crowd dies down. The Judge suddenly reappears and looks down at the motionless figures. Then into the quailing eyes of Faustus.*]

EMPRESS [*uncertainly*]:

We are much beholding to this learned man.

PROSECUTOR:

Now is his fame spread forth in every land.

[*The following happenings are performed with the appropriate National Anthem playing in the background, in a light-hearted revue style.*]

GERMANY:

Military leaders wearing Prussian helmets vigorously shake hands with Faustus. Military line is formed. Formal award-giving ceremony. Golden platter is brought forward. Cover is whipped off to reveal large and ornate beer-stein. This is then whipped off to reveal, underneath, a miniature V2 rocket-bomb. Applause. Cries of 'Heil!', 'Faustus', *etc.*

FRANCE:

Faustus greeted by French legation. Line is formed. All men – except, at end of line, a sultry and voluptuous French tart. Each man quickly and vigorously kisses Faustus on both cheeks (French style). When he gets to tart, expecting the same, she darts out her hand and gives him a brisk, businesslike hand-shake. Cries of 'Vive Faustus!' *etc.*

AMERICA:

Press reception. Ticker tape. Photographers pretend to take photos. President with ten-gallon hat comes forward with gigantic velvet case covered with glittering cover. When whipped off, it reveals two stunning diamond bracelets, which are then put on to a smiling Faustus and clicked shut like handcuffs. With bracelets, still smiling, he raises hands over head for news photos, and gives boxing-champ salute, etc.

ENGLAND:

Formal ceremony. Peers hold open umbrellas as they march. Slow, stately walk towards the Queen (propped up on dais composed of two men back to back, draped with red velvet). Doctor Faustus kneels before the Regent, who is also protected

*by umbrella. She proceeds to dub him. Dubbing sabre suddenly
becomes rubbery and uncontrollable. All panic. Queen topples.
Pandemonium, etc.*

[*After these happenings, Faustus, buoyed up by the adulation, is
discovered alone.*]

GOOD ANGEL [*to Faustus from audience*]:
O gentle Faustus, leave thy damned art.
This magic, that doth charm thy soul to hell,
Will quite bereave thee of salvation.
Repent, repent! Yet will God pity thee.

EVIL ANGEL:
Go forward, Faustus, in that famous art.

GOOD ANGEL:
Sweet Faustus, leave that execrable art.

EVIL ANGEL:
Think of honour and of wealth.

GOOD ANGEL:
Contrition, prayer, repentance –
They are means to bring thee unto heaven.

EVIL ANGEL:
Rather illusions, fruits of lunacy
That make them foolish that do use them most.

GOOD ANGEL:
Sweet Faustus, think of Heaven and of heavenly things.

EVIL ANGEL:
Too late.

GOOD ANGEL:
Never too late.

EVIL ANGEL:
Too late.

GOOD ANGEL:
Never too late.

EVIL ANGEL:
Too late.

FAUSTUS:

Nay, 'tis too late.
My heart is harden'd, I shall ne'er repent;
Scarce can I name salvation, faith, or heaven,
But fearful echoes thunder in mine ears,
'Faustus is damn'd.' Then daggers, swords and knives,
Poison, guns, halters and envenom'd steel
Are laid before me to dispatch myself,
And long ere this I should have done the deed
Had not sweet pleasure conquer'd deep despair.
Have I not made blind Homer sing to me
Of noble Paris' love and Oenon's death?
And hath not he that built the walls of Thebes
With ravishing sound of his melodious harp
Made music with my Mephistophilis?
Why should I die, then, or basely despair?
I'm resolv'd Faustus shall ne'er repent.
Come, Mephistophilis. The restless course
That Time doth run with calm and silent foot
Calls for the payment of my latest years;
Therefore, sweet Mephistophilis, let us
Make haste, to Wittenberg.
    [*Cut to:*]

PROSECUTOR:

Fond worldling, now his heart-blood dries with grief,
His conscience kills it, and his labouring brain
Begets a world of idle fantasies
To overreach the devil; but all in vain;
His store of pleasures must be sauc'd with pain.
Now with his servant Wagner close at hand,
He draws his will and portions out his land.

FAUSTUS [*in study*]:

I have thought upon thee in my Testament, for thou hast
been a trusty servant always unto me. Therefore, ask of me

before I die whate'er thou wilt, and I will give it unto
thee. Come, ask.

WAGNER:

I pray you, let me have your cunning.

FAUSTUS:

I have given thee all my books, upon condition that thou
wouldst not let them be common, but use them for thine
own pleasure and study, and dost thou also desire my
cunning? That mayest thou gain – if thou peruse my books
well.

WAGNER:

But may I also have a spirit for mine own?

FAUSTUS:

Art thou resolv'd?

　[*Wagner nods.*]

Then tell me, in what manner and form wouldst thou have
him?

WAGNER:

In manner and form of an Ape.

FAUSTUS:

Thou shalt have thy Apish spirit, and he shall be bound to
thee as Mephistophilis was to Faustus, but all this upon condition that thou publish my cunning and my conceits with
all that I have done – when I am dead – in an history. So
shall the great acts that I have done be manifest unto the
world.

PROSECUTOR:

Then was Faustus given token of his doom, for he was like
a taken murderer or thief the which findeth himself guilty in
conscience before the Judge hath given sentence; fearing
every hour to die. Greatly was he grieved, and spent the
time talking to himself, wringing of his hands, sobbing and
sighing. He fell away from flesh and kept himself close, and
sometime to ease his disquiet mind he entreated his

companions to his house and there, dissembling, would
sup and be merry.

[*Cut to* FAUSTUS *with Scholars, sharing a joke which when it
subsides sinks Faustus into deep gloom.*]

FIRST SCHOLAR:

Worthy Faustus, methinks your looks are changed.

FAUSTUS:

Oh, gentlemen.

SECOND SCHOLAR:

What ails Faustus?

FAUSTUS:

Ah, my sweet chamber-fellow, had I lived with thee then
had I lived still, but now must die eternally. Look, sirs,
comes he not? Comes he not?

FIRST SCHOLAR:

My dear Faustus, what imports this fear?

SECOND SCHOLAR:

Is all our pleasure turn'd to melancholy?

THIRD SCHOLAR:

He is not well with being over-solitary.

SECOND SCHOLAR:

If it be so, we'll have physicians, and Faustus shall be cured.

THIRD SCHOLAR:

'Tis but a surfeit, sir. Fear nothing.

FAUSTUS:

A surfeit of deadly sin that hath damn'd both body and
soul.

SECOND SCHOLAR:

Yet, Faustus, look up to heaven; remember God's mercies
are infinite.

MEPHISTOPHILIS [*appearing to Faustus only*]:

Now, Faustus, must
Thou needs be damn'd, and canst thou not be sav'd.
What boots it then to think of God or heaven?

Away with such vain fancies and despair;
Despair in God, and trust in Beelzebub.

FAUSTUS:

O gentlemen! Though my heart pant and quiver to remember that I have been a student here these thirty years, oh, would I had never seen Wittenberg, never read a book! and what wonders I have done, all Germany can witness, yea, all the world; for which Faustus hath lost both Germany and the world, yea, heaven itself, heaven, the seat of God, the throne of the blessed, the kingdom of joy; and must remain in hell forever – hell, oh, hell for ever! Sweet friends, what shall become of Faustus being in hell for ever?

SECOND SCHOLAR:

Yet, Faustus, turn to God.

MEPHISTOPHILIS:

To God, He loves thee not;
The god thou serv'st is thine own appetite,
Wherein is fix'd the love of Beelzebub.

FAUSTUS:

Oh, my God, I would weep, but the devil draws in my tears. Gush forth blood, instead of tears. Yea, life and soul! Oh – he stays my tongue. I would lift up my hands, but see, they hold 'em; they hold 'em.

FIRST SCHOLAR:

Who, Faustus?

FAUSTUS:

Lucifer and Mephistophilis. Oh, gentlemen, I gave them my soul for cunning.

LUCIFER [*now illuminated in same area as Mephistophilis*]:

Faustus, we wait upon thy soul,
The time is come which makes it forfeit.

FIRST SCHOLAR:

Why did not Faustus tell us of this before, that divines may have prayed for thee?

FAUSTUS:

Oft have I thought to have done so, but the devil threaten'd
to tear me in pieces if I nam'd God; to fetch me body and
soul if I once gave ear to divinity; and now 'tis too late.
Gentlemen, away; lest you perish with me.

SECOND SCHOLAR:

Oh, what may we do to save Faustus?

FAUSTUS:

Talk not of me, but save yourselves and depart.

THIRD SCHOLAR:

God will strengthen me; I will stay with Faustus.

FIRST SCHOLAR:

Tempt not God, sweet friend, but let us into the next room
and pray for him.

FAUSTUS:

Ay, pray for me, pray for me, gentlemen, farewell; if I live
till morning I'll visit you; if not, Faustus is gone to hell.

MEPHISTOPHILIS:

Faustus, now thou has no hope of heaven.
Therefore despair, think only upon hell,
For that must be thy mansion, there to dwell.

[LUCIFER *and* MEPHISTOPHILIS *fade out.*]

GOOD ANGEL:

O, Faustus, if thou hadst given ear to me
Innumerable joys had follow'd thee;
But thou didst love the world.

EVIL ANGEL:

Gave ear to me,
And now must taste hell's pains perpetually.

GOOD ANGEL:

O, what will all thy riches, pleasures, pomps
Avail thee now?

EVIL ANGEL:

Nothing but vex thee more

To want in hell, that had on earth such store.

[FAUSTUS *now back at Trial.*
The PROSECUTOR *puts down his dossier, and takes a seat behind tribunal table. All sit looking at Faustus.*]

JUDGE:

Oh, thou has lost celestial happiness,
Pleasures unspeakable, bliss without end.
Hadst thou affected sweet divinity,
Hell, or the devil, had no power on thee.
Hadst thou kept on that way, Faustus, think
In what resplendent glory thou hadst sat,
In heavenly throne, like those bright shining saints,
And triumph'd over hell: that hast thou lost;
And now, poor soul, the jaws of hell are open
To receive thee.

FAUSTUS:

Break heart, drop blood, and mingle it with tears,
Tears falling from repentant heaviness
Of thy most vile and loathsome filthiness,
The stench whereof corrupts the inward soul
With such flagitious crimes of heinous sins
As no commiseration may expel,
But mercy, Faustus, of thy Saviour sweet,
Whose blood alone must wash away thy guilt –
Where art thou, Faustus? Wretch, what hast thou done?
Damn'd art thou, Faustus, damn'd; despair and die!

[*Goes to stab himself; is stopped by Monks.*]

FIRST MONK:

Oh, stay, good Faustus, stay thy desperate steps!
I see an angel hover o'er thy head,
And, with a vial full of precious grace,
Offers to pour the same into thy soul:
Then call for mercy, and avoid despair.

FAUSTUS:

I do repent; and yet I do despair;
Hell strives with grace for conquest in my breast.
[*Coming downstage to audience*]
What shall I do to shun the snares of death?
[*The* GOOD *and* EVIL ANGELS *answer Faustus's question,
crying 'Repent' and 'Too Late' respectively. They leave their
seats, climb on to the stage and proceed to have a tug-of-war for
Faustus's Soul. On right of Faustus, all* MONKS *join the
Good Angel. On left* LUCIFER, MEPHISTOPHILIS *and the*
DIPLOMAT *join the Evil Angel. After several tugs, the
forces of evil pull Faustus on to their side, and the forces of
Good, still crying 'Repent', scramble off-stage*]

MEPHISTOPHILIS:

Thou traitor, Faustus, I arrest thy soul
For disobedience to my sovereign lord:
Revolt, or I'll in piece-meal tear thy flesh.

FAUSTUS:

I do repent I e'er offended him.
Sweet Mephistophilis, entreat thy lord
To pardon my unjust presumption,
And with my blood again I will confirm
The former vow I made to Lucifer.

LUCIFER:

Do it, then, Faustus, with unfeigned heart,
Lest greater dangers do attend thy drift.

FAUSTUS [*pointing to Judge, now alone at tribunal table*]:

Torment, sweet friend, that base and aged man
That durst dissuade me from my Lucifer,
With greatest torments that our hell affords.

LUCIFER:

His faith is great; I cannot touch his soul;
But what I may afflict his body with
I will attempt, which is but little worth.

FAUSTUS:

One thing, dread Lord, let me crave of thee,
To glut the longing of my heart's desire –
That I may have unto my paramour
That heavenly Helen which I saw of late,
Whose sweet embraces may extinguish clean
Those thoughts that do dissuade me from my vow,
And keep my oath I made to Lucifer.

LUCIFER:

This, or what else, my Faustus shall desire
Shall be perform'd in twinkling of an eye.
  [*Enter Helen wearing Grecian mask as before.*]

FAUSTUS:

Was this the face that launch'd a thousand ships,
And burnt the topless towers of Ilium?
Sweet Helen, make me immortal with a kiss.
Her lips suck forth my soul: see where it flies! –
Come, Helen, come, give me my soul again.
Here will I dwell, for heaven is in these lips,
And all is dross that is not Helena.
I will be Paris, and for love of thee,
Instead of Troy, shall Wittenberg be sack'd;
And I will combat with weak Menelaus,
And wear thy colours on my plumed crest:
Yea, I will wound Achilles in the heel,
And then return to Helen for a kiss.
Oh, thou art fairer than the evening's air
Clad in the beauty of a thousand stars;
Brighter art thou than flaming Jupiter
When he appear'd to hapless Semele;
More lovely than the monarch of the sky
In wanton Arethusa's azured arms;
And none but thou shalt be my paramour.

  [*As* FAUSTUS *goes to kiss the apparition again, the trial table is suddenly illuminated and all the* MONKS *stand accusingly.*]

JUDGE:

Accursed Faustus, miserable man,
That from thy soul exclud'st the grace of heaven
And fliest the throne of his tribunal seat,
Now art thou damned to hell forever!

[HELEN *suddenly unmasks herself to reveal a triumphant
Mephistophilis.*]

FAUSTUS:

O thou bewitching fiend, 'twas temptation
Hath robb'd me of eternal happiness.

MEPHISTOPHILIS:

I do confess it, Faustus, and rejoice.
'Twas I that, when thou were in the way to heaven,
Damn'd up the passage; when thou took'st the book
To view the scriptures, then I turn'd the leaves
And led thine eyes.
What weep'st thou! 'Tis too late, despair farewell.
Fools that will laugh on earth must weep in hell.

JUDGE [*chanting all on one note*]:

Now, Faustus, let thine eyes with horror stare
Into that vast perpetual torture-house.

SECOND MONK [*chanting*]:

There are the furies, tossing damned souls
On burning forks; their bodies boil in lead.

THIRD MONK [*chanting*]:

There are live quarters broiling on the coals,
That ne'er can die.

FOURTH MONK [*chanting*]:

There, an ever-burning chair
Is for o'er-tortured souls to rest them in.

FIFTH MONK [*chanting*]:

Those that are fed with sops of flaming fire
Were gluttons and lov'd only delicates

And laugh'd to see the poor starve at their gates.

ALL [*chanting*]:

Thou shalt see – ten thousand tortures that more horrid be.

JUDGE:

Now hast thou but one bare hour to live,
And then thou must be damn'd perpetually.

　[*The* MONKS, *whispering prayers for the dead, begin to circle
　Faustus and continue doing so through speech.*]

FAUSTUS:

Stand still, you ever-moving spheres of heaven,
That time may cease and midnight never come;
Fair Nature's eye, rise, rise again and make
Perpetual day; or let this hour be but
A year, a month, a week, a natural day,
That Faustus may repent and save his soul!
Run slowly, slowly, ye steeds of night!

　[*Pause.*]

The stars move still, time runs, the clock will strike,
The devil will come, and Faustus must be damn'd.

VALDES [*chanting*]:

These books, thy wit and our experience
Shall make all nations canonize us.

CORNELIUS [*chanting*]:

Doubt not but to me renown'd.

FAUSTUS:

Oh, I'll leap up to my God! Who pulls me down?

VOICE OF FIRST SCHOLAR:

What ails Faustus?

VOICE OF SECOND SCHOLAR:

He is not well with being over-solitary.

FAUSTUS:

See, see, where Christ's blood streams in the firmament!
One drop would save my soul, half a drop. Ah, my Christ!
Rend not my heart for naming of my Christ!

Yet will I call on him. Oh, spare me, Lucifer ...

FIRST SCHOLAR [*chanting*]:

... he was a scholar, once admir'd

For wondrous knowledge in our German schools ...

FAUSTUS:

Where is it now? 'Tis gone: and see where God

Stretcheth out his arm and bends his ireful brows!

Mountains and hills, come, come and fall on me,

And hide me from the heavy wrath of God!

No, no!

Then will I headlong run into the earth.

Earth, gape! Oh, no, it will not harbour me.

EMPEROR [*chanting*]:

Wonder of men,

EMPRESS [*chanting*]:

Renown'd magician,

EMPEROR [*chanting*]:

Thrice-honoured Faustus.

FAUSTUS:

You stars that reign'd at my nativity,

Whose influence hath allotted death and hell,

Now draw up Faustus, like a foggy mist,

Into the entrails of yon labouring cloud,

That, when you vomit forth into the air,

My limbs may issue from your smoky mouths,

So that my soul may but ascend to heaven.

[*The* MONKS *make the sound of the clock tolling the half-hour.*]

Ah, half the hour is passed: 'twill all be passed anon.

WAGNER:

I think my master shortly means to die

For he hath given to me all his goods.

FAUSTUS:

O God,

If thou wilt not have mercy on my soul,
Yet for Christ's sake, whose blood hath ransom'd me,
Impose some end to my incessant pain;
Let Faustus live in hell a thousand years,
A hundred thousand, and at last be sav'd!
Oh, no end is limited to damned souls!
Why wert thou not a creature wanting soul?
Or why is this immortal that thou hast?
Ah, Pythagoras' 'metempsychosis', were that true,
This soul should fly from me and I be chang'd
Unto some brutish beast; all beasts are happy,
For when they die
Their souls are soon dissolv'd in elements;
But mine must live still to be plagu'd in hell.
Curs'd be the parents that engender'd me!
No, Faustus, curse thyself, curse Lucifer
That hath depriv'd thee of the joy of heaven.

[*Clock (the Monks) begins striking twelve.*]

Oh, it strikes, it strikes! Now, body, turn to air,
Or Lucifer will bear thee quickly to hell!

[*At the twelfth stroke, the circle of Monks stops moving around
Faustus. All stand still and poised.*]

JUDGE:

Cut is the branch that might have grown full straight,
And burned is Apollo's laurel-bough
That sometime grew within this learned man.

FAUSTUS:

O soul, be chang'd into little water-drops,
And fall into the ocean, ne'er be found!

JUDGE:

Faustus is gone!

FAUSTUS:

My God, my God! Look not so fierce on me!
Adders and serpents, let me breathe a while!

JUDGE:
Regard his hellish fall,
Whose fiendful fortune may exhort the wise
Only to wonder at unlawful things,
Whose deepness doth entice such forward wits
To practise more than heavenly power permits.
    [*The circle of Monks slowly begins to tighten around Faustus.*]

FAUSTUS:
Ugly hell, gape not! Come not, Lucifer!
I'LL BURN MY BOOKS.
    [*The circle engulfs Faustus, who is pulled down and disappears
    inside of it. Freeze for a moment. Blackout.*]

MORE ABOUT PENGUINS

Penguinews, which appears every month, contains details of all the new books issued by Penguins as they are published. From time to time it is supplemented by *Penguins in Print,* which is a complete list of all books published by Penguins which are in print. (There are well over three thousand of these.)

A specimen copy of *Penguinews* will be sent to you free on request, and you can become a subscriber for the price of the postage – 4s. for a year's issues (including the complete lists). Just write to Dept EP, Penguin Books Ltd, Harmondsworth, Middlesex, enclosing a cheque or postal order, and your name will be added to the mailing list.

Some other books published by Penguins are described on the following pages.

Note: *Penguinews* and *Penguins in Print* are not available in the U.S.A. or Canada

THE PENGUIN ENGLISH LIBRARY

CHRISTOPHER MARLOWE
THE COMPLETE PLAYS

Edited by J. B. Steane

In recent years there has been a widening of opinion about Marlowe; at one extreme he is considered an atheist rebel and at the other a Christian traditionalist. There is as much divergence in Marlowe's seven plays and, as J. B. Steane says in his introduction, that a man's work should encompass the extremes of *Tamburlaine* and *Edward the Second* is one of the most absorbingly interesting facts of literature; the range of Marlowe's small body of work covers such amazingly unlike pieces as *Doctor Faustus* and *The Jew of Malta*. Controlled and purposeful, these plays contain a poetry which enchants and lodges in the mind.

THE PENGUIN ENGLISH LIBRARY

Planned to take its place alongside the Penguin Classics, this series will eventually include attractive and authoritative editions of the best work to have appeared in English since the fifteenth century.

The following authors are so far represented: Jane Austen, Beckford, Charlotte and Emily Brontë, Bunyan, Samuel Butler, Cobbett, Wilkie Collins, Congreve, Defoe, Dickens, George Eliot, Etherege, Fielding, Gissing, Samuel Johnson, Ben Jonson, Marlowe, Melville, Meredith, Middleton, Poe, Mary Shelley, Smollett, Sterne, Swift, Thackeray, Tourneur, Trollope, Twain, Walpole, Webster, and Wycherley.

THE NIGEL BARTON PLAYS
Dennis Potter

Dennis Potter's award-winning television comedies are almost savage in the irony they extract from British politics. *Stand Up, Nigel Barton,* the first play, shows his central character contemplating politics as a career – having been a misfit at home, at school and at Oxford. In the second play, *Vote Vote Vote for Nigel Barton,* against a background of intrigue he is a candidate in a rural election, fighting a losing battle in a 'safe' opposition seat. The plays read brilliantly and Dennis Potter has provided a hard-hitting introduction in which he assesses the situation of those writing seriously for television today.